SIMPLY OWN IT!

The American Dream

Increase Wealth with Commercial Real Estate

Andrea Davis, CCIM

 FriesenPress

One Printers Way
Altona, MB R0G 0B0
Canada

www.friesenpress.com

ISBN
978-1-03-917467-2 (Hardcover)
978-1-03-917466-5 (Paperback)
978-1-03-917468-9 (eBook)

1. BUSINESS & ECONOMICS, REAL ESTATE

Distributed to the trade by The Ingram Book Company

This book is dedicated to those who strive to make our world a better place for others.

This includes my husband, daughter and two pups.

Life is better because of you.

ACKNOWLEDGMENTS

A special thank you to the following friends and colleagues whom without this project would have stalled, crashed and burned.

JoLee Kennedy and Jan Hanson, fellow authors, editors and members of North Scottsdale Critique Group. Without the last few years of monthly late-night edits, redlines and lengthy critique sessions this book would not have seen the light of day. I am ever grateful for the encouragement, seriousness and dedication to our craft.

Patricia L. Brooks, friend and founder of Scottsdale Society for Women Writers and its authors who inspired me and still inspire me toward the dream, and to persevere with excellence.

Robert leger, my editor who made SimpLEASEity read like honey and Dwight Getting, my branding guru and book cover designer.

Industry specialists Jennifer Langford and Dana McDonald with Stewart Title and Trust and Drew Schnackenberg with First Western Trust.

And the Davis Commercial AZ Team. Christine Juby, Quentin Hick, David Roberson, Cathy Maloney and Stuart Davis.

Family, friends and clients who shared their insight, wisdom and experience generously. Especially, my loving and devoted husband Stuart (responsible for the book name) and daughter Mikella who together patiently endured and supported the entire process.

Thank you!

CONTENTS

PART I

Building Equity in *Your* Future

INTRODUCTION

From birth, my fate as a third-generation American meant acquiring property, and if luck would have it, owning my own business. Rooted in the American dream, my four siblings and I were taught that ownership equaled success. "Dream big! You can do anything you put your mind to," was my parents' mantra.

Growing up in a Midwestern family, our Sunday afternoon ritual involved exploring new homes being built in the neighborhood and following the progress until completion. We would tour older houses and envision their renovations. Eventually, my parents bought a farm with a two-story 200-year-old log cabin, which became our family project to renovate into the twenty-first century. This simple act instilled in me that property ownership offered freedoms that only the very wealthy enjoyed in other countries. Ownership in the United States equaled wealth and a comfortable retirement.

My passion for real estate started with homes and expanded to commercial real estate. My commercial real estate specialty was selling speculative office condominium projects, where business owners and professionals would commit to buying a speculative building, a portion of it or a piece of dirt. Marketing building ownership with a rendering and site plan was the challenge. The condo developer needed 40 percent presales to secure the construction loan. Until over 40 percent of the project was under contract and in escrow, the project sat dormant, unable to proceed. Selling spec office condos was no easy task, and a paycheck could be as far out as two years.

Once the developer broke ground, the remaining 60 percent of the project magically became "real" to business owners, and the balance of the project sold quickly. A broker's commission is paid after the whole project is completed and title is transferred to the new owner. One needs a strong faith in ownership to patiently wait two years for a paycheck. My belief in the American dream of small-business real estate ownership made it possible to successfully presell proposed business parks. In the local brokerage world, I was quickly dubbed "the Office Condo Queen."

Contracting with a developer to sell office condos, I soon realized that the business owner seldom understood complex commercial purchase requirements. As a result, a buyer who didn't have adequate representation was at a severe disadvantage and usually paid more for the property than necessary.

When I opened my own brokerage firm, I shifted my focus to assist buyers through the purchase process, establishing a successful nine-step process to owning a commercial building.

My Commercial Purchase Experience

Most of this book educates the buyer on the commercial real estate transaction process. When I purchased my own office, the choices I made throughout the transaction were based on experience, intimate knowledge of the market, strong third-party relationships, and a love for the property I found. My passion and commitment to own this property, balanced with years of transactional knowledge, allowed me to make rapid decisions that led to my ideal property purchase.

It takes expertise to purchase commercial property. My hope is that, by sharing my personal purchase experience as well as knowledge gained by representing hundreds of buyers, I can educate business owners on the ins and outs of the transaction. But before I explain the expedited nine-step process in depth, I present my own office condo experience.

My virtual commercial real estate business had outgrown the home office. After a decade of operating remotely, our team needed a collaborative community environment to propel the business to the next level. My goal was to buy an office building within twelve to eighteen months. Over my commercial tenure of twenty plus years, I assisted hundreds of companies in purchasing their ideal commercial building. I knew exactly how to accomplish my dream. As fate would have it, my search did not take the normal path that this nine-step book outlines. Having gone through these steps with so many clients, I was able to roll with the expedited flow and come out a winner.

The Search

My office search ended before it began.

I had a routine listing presentation scheduled with an experienced business owner to discuss the right time to sell their two office condos. We sat down at the conference table in the clean but outdated 2,040-square-foot tri-plex office condo built in the 1980s, and discussed the value of the obsolete real estate.

The office was boring and butt ugly. The more we discussed sale expectations, the more my imagination expanded and envisioned the space as the coolest office ever. It had enormous potential to become a stunning and efficient work setting.

The Offer

By now I had delivered a spot-on listing presentation. We discussed market conditions and that the market was climbing in the seller's favor. I said, "We should push the property comparables and list the property high. I'm sure we'll have an interested buyer within a week and possibly get the full asking price."

I was on a roll and had the sellers captivated. Their pen hovered over the listing agreement, eager to sign on the dotted line. Then the light bulb went off for me and emotion stomped on logic. I did exactly what I advise clients not to do: *I fell in love with that butt ugly office.* Sometimes, it just happens, and the buyer must go with the flow. This time the buyer just happened to be me.

This was my office condo! The one I had dreamed of for ten years and now, thanks to my energetic presentation, I was faced with paying over market value to secure my future.

My mind backpedaled to figure out how I could negotiate against my broker self or convince the seller to sell to me at a lesser value. I'm sure you know how that went down. I ended up paying top dollar for the unit that required a total renovation. They were happy, and now I had to scramble. It was worth it, as this unit was in hot demand. I had a handful of buyers who would gratefully pay full asking.

Again, the nine-step process saved me.

The Negotiation

I had recently sold two of the ten office condos in the complex and knew its assets and deficits . This office condo project, an uncut diamond in north Scottsdale, was undervalued by brokers, appraisers, and sellers. The market had not discovered this forgotten gem. Recent rezoning favored growth, and that meant values were sure to rise.

I did not want this property going to market just to have to bid against another buyer who felt my passion. Yet as a licensed real estate broker, I had a responsibility to a potential client, and now I was faced with a conflict of interest. By law, and by ethics, the seller had to be treated honestly and fairly and understand the true market value of their property. After expressing my desire to purchase the suite, I suggested they hire a different commercial broker to aid them in the transaction. Having bought and sold a considerable amount of real estate, the owner felt comfortable using only one broker, me. This was written into the contract.

Together we negotiated the subsequent win-win deal. This is the ultimate goal of any transaction, a deal where both parties smile at closing.

Concessions

The seller needed a flexible closing date to coincide with their new office renovation. Already ahead of the goal to own by twelve months, agreeing to a flexible closing date was an easy compromise. From a previous buyer's building inspections on a similar unit, I understood the project inside and out. There were no serious structural issues. The due diligence period, or inspection time, was shortened to two weeks instead of the customary four to six weeks. After those two weeks, a significant earnest money deposit became non-refundable. If for some reason I canceled escrow and did not close on the property, these funds would automatically be released to the seller.

Additionally, I reduced my broker's commission from 6 percent to 3 percent, enhancing the seller's yield. It was a win-win for the seller and for me, the buyer. At the close of escrow, I received a credit for my commission, which reduced the actual cost of the building, but the Affidavit of Sale remained high and increased the neighborhood comparables. This was important to the seller since they planned to sell the second office condo within six months, and they wanted top value for that unit.

Successful negotiations meet each party's needs.

The Lender

Through many years in the industry, I had built solid lender relationships, which secured remarkable terms for my buyers and closed transactions in record time when required. I reached out to a choice few and they pulled through for me as well. Within days, prequalification terms were met, and I was assured we could close in a flexible time frame. Owning my first commercial property was on the horizon.

Fate stepped in. A favorite client sought to relocate his home office and asked if I would consider a fifty-fifty partnership in the building. My company only needed the bottom floor, and my partner wanted the top floor, a natural fit. Ironically, we originally met at this complex.

My new partner was open to traditional bank financing, paying all cash, or acting as the lender with favorable terms. However, the partnership allowed us to pay cash for both the property and the renovation. Had I gone alone, I would have chosen to finance the purchase, yet paying cash gave me comfort in a volatile economy.

The Buildout

Prior to the expiration of a buyer's due diligence period, it is prudent to know the buildout cost for financing and budgeting. My partner had recently renovated two homes, and I had assisted clients in commercial renovations throughout the years, so we had a good idea of what our taste in design would cost. We budgeted seventy-five to one hundred dollars per square foot for the modern office renovation. Our new neighbor in the complex, dubbed "Budgetless Doug," was completing his over-the-top renovation for one hundred dollars per square foot. Surely, for our general office use, even with rising costs, our renovation expense would be under that number.

We were in for a surprise two months later after we approved the architectural drawings and started the construction bidding process. Despite my connections within the industry, the first construction bids came in at $250 per square foot. I nearly collapsed. The prior year, a surgery center would not have cost this much to build out. Five additional bids from reliable contractors ranged from $150–$250 per square foot (PSF). The price increase in this two-month period was staggering.

The perfect economic storm continued to stress the construction industry in Arizona. Demand for commercial product soared, labor shortages plagued the construction trade, and the supply chain of goods broke. Clients in logistics and manufacturing warned us of hyperinflation and advised us to purchase all of our finishes, fixtures, and furniture immediately—even before demolition. We considered holding off on the buildout for a year, but we did not see a slowdown in construction for a few years. We chose to bite the bullet. Fortunately, even paying top dollar, we had bought the property low enough to justify a high remodeling price.

Our relationships, experience, and insider advice saved us numerous time delays and thousands of dollars, helping us to stay on budget once we hired a contractor.

Without a partner to share in the higher costs, I might have panicked and bailed on my dream office. But in the end, even with our remodel doubling in cost, the property stayed within the market value. Now we enjoy the benefits and pride of ownership in a showcase office. And so can you.

The Financial Planner and CPA

The decision to purchase an office included discussions with our financial planner and CPA from the start. Increased company profits opened opportunities for different write-offs, one being an office building. Our company and personal CPA assured us that whether the condo was bought with cash or financed, we would have tax benefits. Since the unit was a total remodel, *cost segregation* depreciation was incorporated in our tax planning. Our financial picture included an exit strategy for the office condo.

Industry Lingo: *Cost segregation* is a strategic tax planning tool that allows companies to increase cash flow by accelerating depreciation deductions and deferring federal and state income taxes after construction in commercial real estate. It can reduce depreciation from thirty-nine years to five years.

There are numerous ways to take title of a property at the close of escrow. Our CPA and financial planner advised us to purchase the office building with a new Limited Liability Company, (LLC). Additionally, our 50 percent of ownership in the LLC would be held by our family trust since we planned on holding the asset for years. This plan would benefit our legacy and keep the property out of probate.

The Team

Buying any commercial property takes an experienced team, favorable market conditions, and patience. With guidance and practical tips gleaned from years of practice, any buyer can simply and successfully accomplish property ownership and realize the American Dream.

This is why I wrote *Simply Own It*.

Oh, my new nickname? "Budgetless Andy."

Before, During, and After Office Condo PHOTOS:

8160 E Butherus - Office Condo Tri-plex 1990s Design

8160 E Butherus - Gutted Tri-plex Office Condo

Andrea Davis

8160 E Butherus - Remodeled Seven Months Later

Ownership Value

Ownership builds equity in *your* future, not your landlord's. An owner reaps greater tax benefits, has an avenue to save for tomorrow, and is empowered with the pride of ownership. Best of all, business owners control their destiny and add to their retirement plan.

Book one of this series, *SimpLEASEity*™, summarizes the complex lease transaction in nine easy steps. Book two, *Simply Own It, the American Dream*, details timing of ownership in this simple guidebook. Throughout the nine step process we will:

1. Answer important questions relevant to commercial real estate purchasing.

2. Evaluate owners' options: should I lease or purchase, and when?

3. Explore the tax benefits of ownership.

4. Offer money-saving strategies when purchasing a building.

5. Outline select professionals who support your dream of commercial real estate ownership.

6. Describe the differences between build-to-suit, spec building, and second-generation building.

7. Discuss exit strategies: When should I sell, and why?

My company, Davis Commercial AZ, is ranked among the top ten office brokerage firms in the Phoenix Metropolitan Area. My goal is to share commercial real estate secrets that save companies time, energy, and money while preparing them for the future.

While a portion of my business facilitates lease negotiations for business owners, my favorite part of brokerage is acquisitions and dispositions. I have sold millions of dollars of *owner/user* commercial buildings and investment properties, supporting companies that want to invest in themselves and the American Dream.

Industry Lingo: An *owner/user* or *owner-occupied* building is typically defined as a property where a company locates its business and occupies at least half of the space.

For me, the American Dream is property ownership. It's a no brainer. Ownership pays, provided you have a plan in place and analyze the odds. Why not put some of that rent in your own pocket instead of making your landlord richer?

Ownership—It Pays

This book removes the mystery of purchasing commercial space and helps you understand the many steps involved when buying a building for your business. *Simply Own It* contains confidence-building tools that empower buyers to negotiate a successful purchase contract, hire competent buyer representation, and take advantage of insider secrets to avoid problems and save money.

The first action you need to take when considering a commercial building purchase is hiring a qualified professional—a buyer representative—*to protect your interests*. That's what Zak did when he negotiated a purchase price of $1,265,400 (or $225 PSF) for his dream office building. The office condo unit, 5,624 SF, had gorgeous appointments, a great floor plan, and a walk-in bank vault—perfect for his cannabis business.

During his homework phase, his *buyer representative* discovered that three of the eleven reserved covered parking spaces allocated to the suite had been used by the neighbor for eight years. Additionally, the suite size was recorded differently in three key places: on the *plat map*, within the final *covenants, conditions, and restrictions, (CC&R's)* and on the county assessor's official website. This discrepancy of over one hundred SF could have added $22,500 to the purchase price.

Industry Lingo: Buyer Representative/Buyer Rep is a real estate professional who guides buyers through the process of purchasing a property.

Industry Lingo: Plat Map is a document drawn to scale by a licensed Engineer or Surveyor, showing the divisions of a piece of land.

Industry Lingo: Covenants, conditions and restrictions or CC&Rs are a set of rules governing the use of a certain piece of real estate in a given community.

Fortunately, Zak had hired an experienced *buyer rep* who walked everyone through the steps necessary to determine the correct suite square footage and how to recover the "stolen" parking spaces.

Guess how much this personal advisor cost him? Not one cent. Read on to find out why this is the best value you'll ever get. Even if you remain determined to represent yourself when buying commercial property, this handbook will help you learn how to use market knowledge to improve your commercial real estate negotiation skills.

Nine Steps to Ownership

The first portion of this book discusses the basics of commercial real estate, the attributes of a skilled buyer representative, and how to qualify them. The second portion outlines the nine-step purchase process in detail showing examples of how a buyer (like you!) navigates their way through the intricate process.

Step One—Strategic plan, the power of preparation.

Step Two—Identify potential properties.

Step Three—Property tour, seeing is believing.

Step Four—Patience, the letter of intent.

Step Five—The lender and due diligence.

Step Six—The title company.

Step Seven—Design and construction bidding process.

Step Eight—The home stretch, the close.

Step Nine—Ownership, one task at a time.

At the end of this guidebook, for easy reference, is a list of industry definitions, a streamlined checklist of the purchase process, a buyer purchase matrix, a checklist for hiring both buyer rep and attorney, and top buyer mistakes when purchasing a building.

The beginning of each chapter includes a list of keywords. Pop outs stress valuable tips for readers throughout the book including:

Timeline: The estimated time each phase of the process takes.

$$$ Saving Tip: Signals a money saving tip.

Industry Lingo: Terminology used in the industry.

Business Owner Tip: Helps buyers make educated, informed location decisions.

Do The Math: Provides an industry calculation to assist with financial modeling.

Now, let's begin.

CHAPTER 1

Commercial Real Estate *(CRE)* Basics

Keywords: SBA, lending, commercial real estate, big business, buyer, seller, developer, lender, asking rate, investment, office condos, fee simple

---

Industry Lingo: *CRE* is a widely used industry acronym for *commercial real estate*.

Before the nine-steps of purchasing can be executed, it's necessary to understand a few CRE fundamentals. The key to property ownership success is twofold:

1. Understand how CRE fundamentals fit into the larger scheme of a purchase.

2. Recognize the importance of retaining experienced buyer representation and other CRE professionals to save money on your new commercial building.

Ownership is a Privilege

Ownership of property is a luxury that is not a universal right. Even in the U.S. most small to midsize business owners haven't been able to enjoy the pride of commercial property ownership for two reasons: lending and availability of product. In this chapter we briefly discuss both.

Making loans affordable

The Small Business Administration (SBA) was the brainchild of President Herbert Hoover in 1932. It was designed for small businesses to participate and stay competitive in the marketplace. In 1954, SBA started offering U.S. government guaranteed bank loans to small businesses. By the late 1980s, the popularity of SBA loans opened acquisition opportunities for small business owners, enabling them to control their expenses through a monthly mortgage.

Prior to SBA financing, commercial loans had higher interest rates, required 20 to 40 percent down, and offered only a five-year fixed interest rate, even though the loan was amortized over twenty to twenty-five years. The lender's risk mirrored the tenant's lease term, and after five years, the loan had to be renegotiated.

This five-year loan structure was unpredictable for small business owners, and they did not want the risk of new lending terms every five years. Conversely, lenders did not want to bank on small business owners who might experience economic hardship during difficult times.

The creation of SBA loans opened the door for banks to take more risk on smaller commercial real estate loans because the U.S. government partially backs the loan. In case of default by the borrower, the loss suffered by the lender is reduced. The SBA allows business owners to finance commercial real estate at reasonable interest rates for longer periods. We will discuss commercial lending at length in a future chapter.

Office Condominiums

Another factor empowering small businesses to own rather than rent their offices, was the advent of *office condominium* projects in the 1990s. Developers had overbuilt, and office users were downsizing. To liquidate overbuilt inventory and reduce financial liability, developers sold the buildings in sections as condominiums. Ownership was born to the small business owner.

Industry Lingo: *Office condominium* or *office condo* is defined as an office building with two or more individually owned units.

Office/retail/industrial condo ownership works similarly to residential condominiums. Terms of ownership are outlined in office condo association covenants, conditions, restrictions (*CC&Rs*), and by-laws. The exterior of the property is managed by the association. Generally, an outside firm is hired to manage the property and run it as a multi-buyer office building. The rest of the property (i.e., the parking lot, easements, landscape, and lobby) is owned in common and equally shared by all condo owners. The condo associations has specific CC&R's, bylaws, and articles of incorporation to assure each owners' property values remain intact.

Industry Lingo: *CC&Rs* are limits and rules placed on a condominium complex by a builder, developer, and office property association.

Fee Simple Property

Fee simple property ownership is the best type of ownership because the owner(s) can do whatever they like to the property subject to zoning, encumbrances, local guidelines, etc. The property owner is not subject to an office condo association's rules and regulations.

Other Ownership Options

Other ways to accomplish the dream of ownership are:

1. Acquire land and custom build your own office building. This route takes the most planning, time, and in most cases, money.

2. Buy a residential home where the municipality will allow commercial zoning. The zoning process takes time and often involves an attorney.

3. Purchase a building larger than your company needs and lease out the balance of the space.

Business Owner Tip: If your tenant vacates, have sufficient funds available to cover any property maintenance costs.

Next Steps

With a few commercial real estate basics now under our belt, we can define the pros and cons of purchasing versus leasing. In chapter two, we examine when to buy and why.

CHAPTER 2

Lease Versus Purchase

Am I a Candidate to Buy?

Aaron has a decision to make. His successful naturopathic office is housed in a 5,000-square-foot commercial building that he leases. Aaron bought the practice from his mentor, who founded the business on this property. Neighbors view the business as an icon within their community. Aaron plans to practice here for another twenty years.

The building owner, Harmel, hired me to sell the property to Aaron, the current tenant, or another investor. It sits in a good neighborhood, with strong demographics for Aaron's practice. His lease expires in four years.

The building should sell quickly in the current seller's market. In my opinion, Aaron is the natural buyer. With the seller's permission, I meet with Aaron to explain the building sale and the implications to his business.

"Aaron, as you're aware, Harmel is intent on selling this building. Once the building transfers ownership, no lease terms will change except who you pay rent to. However, because you don't have an option to extend after four years, the new owner could raise your rent to whatever the market will stomach. I've seen new owners take advantage of renewing a doctor's lease, because a doctor can lose up to 15–20 percent of their patient base when they relocate."

"That doesn't sound good for me," Aaron says. "I hope I don't have to move, for a multitude of reasons. Is there anything I can do to protect myself?"

"You have two options. The first is to ask Harmel to extend your lease before he sells the building, so you know what your rental rate is for the next seven to ten years. This way a new owner can't push you out if they find a buyer willing to pay a higher rent. Harmel will like this because commercial real estate investors like long term leases."

Aaron sighs in relief and leans back in his chair. "That sounds positive and reasonable."

"Another option," I continue, "is for you to buy the building and control your destiny."

The expression on Aaron's face says this is a lot for him to take in. He rubs his temples, and then finally responds. "I'm not sure about buying a commercial building right now. I just bought a new home. I doubt I can get financing."

I respectfully interrupt, "You have three years of profitable business under your belt and a track record of paying monthly rent payments that are higher than your mortgage would be. Ownership allows you to control your monthly payments, provides tax benefits, and builds equity. Lenders love doctors."

"My dream is to own my building," Aaron confesses.

"Not to overwhelm you, but in the future, when your business sells, you can hold the real estate as an investment property with a monthly income or sell the building and invest in something else."

I tap away at my retro HP 10BII calculator. "Let me confirm that your estimated monthly mortgage payment would indeed be less than your rent."

Interest rates are in Aaron's favor, and he can save over $1,000 each month with only 10 percent down. With the right lender, he might even qualify for zero percent down.

Just like that, Aaron's decision is simplified. Purchasing appears to be the best option, and he is determined to capitalize on the opportunity.

The result: Aaron secures a loan with zero down and monthly mortgage payments below his previous rent. Down the road Aaron plans to sell his practice and lease the building to the new business owner, shifting the property to a retirement investment. The seller receives 98 percent of his asking price and a quick close. Everybody wins.

There are as many reasons to buy property as there are businesses.

- Margaret bought a building for her insurance company to be part of her children's inheritance. Her family trust bought the building and the company paid rent to the trust.

- Stuart bought a property for his steel company as a built-in savings plan for his baby girl's college education. "I can sell the property in eighteen years to fund her college. My wife and I sleep better at night knowing her education is handled."

- Charles bought a huge warehouse for his truck-ing company because he wanted to retire in ten

years; owning the warehouse will double his retirement savings.

- Deborah bought her orthodontics office because of
the high buildout cost of her interior space. She knew
a landlord would only contribute to a portion of the
buildout. She was determined to invest that capital in
her business versus a landlord's pocket. "This location
will be my home until I sell my practice in twenty-five
years. Then I will revisit whether to sell the building
with the practice or remain a landlord and receive a
monthly income," she said.
- Chris, owner of a cheer/gymnastics school, was tired
of being at the landlord's mercy. "Even though I negotiated a good lease, I still had to pay for everything that
went wrong in my place. I felt like I was constantly
being nickel and dimed, and I was not in control of
anything. I'm buying to control my future."

There are many reasons to purchase a building to run your business,
yet timing is essential. If a company buys too early in its business cycle, it
may not have enough money for payroll, inventory, or other essential business components. If a company buys too late in its business life, flexibility
to sell at the optimum time to maximize a return on investment may be
limited. A property owner ideally wants to sell when the market is in their
favor—a seller's market.

Timing is Everything

The best time to purchase a commercial building varies. Most often, timing
depends on multiple factors, such as a company's business philosophy,

its business cycle of economic expansion and contraction, and its financial strength.

It is normal to struggle when deciding to buy or continue leasing. Matt's young business, Style Luxury Homes, is thriving due to its impeccable reputation. The lease, with a three-year option to renew, is up for renewal. Since Matt first signed, market rents have increased, and his rent will jump 20 percent despite the generous "below market" lease rate offered by the landlord. Compared to other lease options, the new rates and terms are fair. In the open market, the landlord could demand more.

The landlord knows it is in her interest to have Matt take the extension, allowing her to avoid the headache of finding another reliable tenant. The landlord has learned that the real cost of securing a new tenant far exceeds what she's giving up with her discounted rental rate for an extension.

She also sees another option. And timing may be on Matt's side.

The landlord wants to capitalize on a seller's market that has real estate prices at an all-time high. She asks Matt if he is interested in purchasing the office building at $250 per square foot. Commercial ownership intrigues Matt and seems like a good fit for the company. He knows the unit is in a rare, high-demand location and, most importantly, close to his customer base.

Matt and his partner believe in ownership yet hesitate. In 2008, the company barely survived the downturn, and this experience cements a conservative business plan. Ideally, Matt had planned to lease for one more year, and then purchase.

Let us review the math for Style Luxury Homes and help Matt make his decision.

DO THE MATH:

Building Size: 5,500 SF

Purchase Price: $250 per square foot (SF) annually = $1,375,000

Back of the Napkin Mortgage Calculation

Assumptions: 10% down, 5% interest, amortized over 25 years

Purchase Price: $1,375,000

10% Down: $137,500

Loan Amount: $1,237,500

Monthly Mortgage Payment: **$7,234.00** or $15.78 per square foot annually with NO annual rent escalations like a lease.

Lease Calculation

New NNN Lease Rate: $20 per square foot annually. (This rent value is net all building expenses in order to compare apples to apples.)

Monthly Lease Rate: $20 SF x 5,500 / 12 = **$9,167** (with 3% annual increases)

What would you do if you had the down payment amount?

Style Luxury Homes will save over $120,000 over five years by purchasing their own building. That nearly $2,000 a month savings in rent provides Style Luxury Homes the confidence to purchase the building and weather a potential future economic crisis.

Tools to Determine Your Next Step

Analytical spreadsheets are useful tools that can be as simple or complicated as buyers want. Below is an Excel spreadsheet with changeable cells
to determine if purchasing a building will cost more or less than leasing.
This simple tool can compare monthly expenditures apples to apples. Your
buyer rep, CPA, or financial planner can help with this analysis. (Or go to my
website, www.davisCREAZ.com, and request the Excel form.)

Lease Versus Purchase Analysis

Lease Costs

Gross Lease Basis	$24.00
Expense Stop	$0.00
NNN Basis	$24.00
Inflation Factor	3.00%
Square Footage	10,500
Annual Lease Payments	$252,000
Monthly Lease Payments	$21,000
Additional TI Financing	$0
TOTAL MO. LEASE COSTS	**$21,000**

Ownership/Mortgage Calculation

Building Square Footage	10,500	
Building Price/Square Foot	$275	
Tenant Improvements	$15	
Building Cost		$3,045,000
Down Payment	10%	$304,500
Amount Financed		$2,740,500
Interest Rate	4.25%	
Loan Term (Yr)	25	
Annual Mortgage Payments		$180,091
Monthly Mortgage Payments		$15,008
TIs financed		$0
TOTAL MO. MORTGAGE COSTS		**$15,008**

Total Purchase Price

Building Price/Square Foot	$275	$2,887,500
Building Square Footage	10,500	
Tenant Improvements	$15	$157,500
Building Cost		$3,045,000

Accumulated Savings Over 10 Years *

Sale		Year
Sales Price (Net)		$3,045,000
Exit Year	10	$1,967,765
Cumulative Cashflow	0	$0
Net Savings/(Loss)		**$1,077,235**

Lease Assumptions

Estimated NNNs	$9.00
Annual increases	3%

Additional Purchase Costs

+ Association estimate:	$2.75 SF Annually
+ Property taxes estimate:	$2.75 SF Annually
+ Utilities & janitorial estim:	$2.50 SF Annually
	$8

Financial components that make up the triple nets (NNN)
Sales Transaction does NOT include tax benefits or appreciation of real estate.

Reasons to Consider a Purchase:

1. Your long-term business plan includes commercial real estate ownership.

2. Part of your company exit plan is selling the business and holding the real estate as an annuity.

3. Business growth supports buying a building to offset financial gains. In other words, your CPA says you need additional tax write-offs.

4. The landlord will pay only a portion of a substantial property remodel. You, as the tenant, must cover the balance of the expense. Businesses with extensive buildout costs include medical, dental, imaging centers, restaurants, and manufacturing companies.

Right Time to Buy

The right time to purchase a building varies from company to company. It depends on a company's long-term goals, its exit strategy, financial health, and product inventory.

Remember Chris, who runs the cheer/gymnastic company and wants to control his rental expense future? His business is busting at the seams with 300 kids and a wait list. Chris's business is in a high growth area, where new homes are popping up in every direction. Commercial buildings lag the growth spurt. He needs either warehouse or retail space with high ceilings and wide-open bays. Neither exist in a reasonable size to purchase. For Chris to fulfill his vision, he will need to buy land and build from the ground up. This new venture can distract from the business and take up to two years to complete.

Is the wait worth the hassle and distraction of building? Can his business continue to thrive in a holding pattern for two years? Because Chris cannot find a location to lease for his expansion, and because he needs to expand, he answers both questions with a yes. A *build-to-suit* will be required.

Industry Lingo: A *build-to-suit* is an agreement between the developer and the buyer to construct a building specifically for the buyer.

The infographic below is designed to help a buyer decide when it is an advantageous time to purchase a building.

BUSINESS CYCLE	RIGHT TIME	WRONG TIME
Your business is taking a new direction or growing.	Probably not.	The new business model is untested. Save your capital for the business growth.
Your business is downsizing.	If your business has stabilized at the reduced size, yes.	If your business downsized due to insufficient funds, no.
There is liquidity and extra money to spend.	Yes, under most circumstances.	No, if your company is growing each year.
You are determined to be your own landlord.	Yes, provided your company growth has slowed or you purchase extra space for future growth.	The company is stretched financially. Property ownership requires cash on hand just like home ownership.
Your business partnership disintegrated and there is an opportunity to buy the building.	Yes, if the partner wants to sell the building for a market price or below.	No, if your partner is going to rake you over the coals.
Pandemic or mandatory government closures.	Yes, provided your business remains unaffected and enjoys strong cash flow. Negotiations may benefit the buyer.	Business restructuring is required. It is advantageous to stabilize a business prior to a building purchase, otherwise you may be spending money on a mortgage versus on your immediate business demands.

The pros and cons of purchasing are personal and specific to each business. Purchase pros and cons are outlined separately to decide if purchasing is the right action for your business. Rank each pro and con with a value from zero to four (zero being insignificant, and four being important) to see which plan of action supports your business.

Pros to Purchase a Building:

- ☐ Control your destiny. You don't have to ask a landlord for permission to make changes.
- ☐ Stabilized mortgage payment year after year.
- ☐ Sell the asset with the business, or lease it to the new business owner for income.
- ☐ Tax benefits.
- ☐ Appreciation of asset—increased property value over time.
- ☐ Rental income—have secondary income from other renters. Keep in mind if you have a Small Business Administration loan, you are required to occupy 51 percent of the building.
- ☐ Pride of ownership.

Cons to Purchase a Building:

- ☐ Generally, upfront costs are higher when buying. Anticipate 10—20 percent of the purchase price versus first and last month's rent payment upon lease signing.
- ☐ Building owners are responsible for all property maintenance.
- ☐ In a down market, the landlord may decrease your annual rent. A lender will require your established mortgage payments.
- ☐ Loss of liquidity. If you can't sell the building, you're stuck with it until a buyer comes along. You could lose money.
- ☐ If things turn for the worse, a foreclosure stays on your credit report for up to seven years.
- ☐ Property values may have declined when it is your time to sell.

SIMPLY OWN IT!

☐ Buyers need upfront capital, management, and patience.

☐ Often a landlord will contribute to buyer improvement costs.

☐ Prepayment penalties often apply to a loan if the property is sold within a certain time frame.

CHAPTER 3
The Cost of Buyer Representation

Keywords: broker, agent, listing broker, buyer rep, Realtors®, agency law, legal obligation, fiduciary duty, fair and truthful, listing agreement, commission cost, purchase contract, fully executed, house, in-house, off-market, rent abatement

Brokers: Beware

Don't be fooled! Many buyers confuse a seller's broker for *their* representative. Inexperienced buyers can easily mistake the person showing the commercial buildings as someone who will take care of them in purchase negotiations. They don't, and here's why: Sellers want to make money, and buyers want to save money.

The seller's broker has a fiduciary duty to the seller or the building owner, so representing the buyer fairly is next to impossible. A single broker can't feasibly represent both sides of a transaction.

When a seller's broker insists on representing both buyer and seller, beware! Your interests as the buyer will not come first.

Titles Matter: Agent Versus Broker

Commercial real estate sales agents are often incorrectly referred to as brokers. Technically, a real estate broker has a designation based on state laws that exceeds an agent's level of responsibility. This applies to both residential and commercial brokerage. Brokers often hire agents to work under them. In CRE, these agents are known as:

- Listing agent/broker or seller's agent/broker. They are retained by the seller for representation.
- Agent/broker or Buyer's agent/broker represents the building buyer.
- Most CRE brokers/agents are not Realtors®. The Realtor® trademark is a designation indicating membership in the National Association of Realtors® which focuses on residential real estate. It's rare that residential agents have training or experience in the complexities of CRE transactions. It's best not to trust your commercial real estate leasing or purchase to a residential specialist.

The Real World

In the real world, buyer/seller representation isn't black and white. At times, brokers specialize in representing either buyers or sellers. Large commercial brokerages separate duties to minimize legal liability. For instance,

Cushman & Wakefield has a division of brokers who only represent sellers, and a separate division for buyer reps.

Medium-size brokerage companies often allow a broker to provide seller or buyer representation on different transactions. They may discourage one broker from representing both seller and broker in a single transaction to avoid liability issues.

In smaller communities, however, there often isn't a choice, and brokers may have to work both sides of a transaction. Brokers are required to fully disclose any conflicts of interest, such as if a property is controlled by the broker's company. The broker code requires fair and truthful disclosure to all parties. When a buyer elects to work with a broker representing both sides of the building sale transaction, it is even more crucial to understand the nine steps of purchasing.

Business Owner Tip: If a listing broker shows a property(s) without your buyer rep alongside, inform the listing broker you are working with buyer representation. Ideally, instruct your buyer rep to set up the tour so the lines of representation are clear from the get-go.

The Ease of Legalese

A broker is legally bound to a seller after a listing agreement contract is signed. The broker's fiduciary duty is to provide the highest standard of care to their client, the building owner. The same is true for buyer representation.

- A listing agreement is between a building seller and a listing broker.
- A buyer representation contract, or employment contract, is between a buyer and the buyer rep.

When the listing broker helps both seller and buyer negotiate a purchase contract, the broker's legal obligation is to the seller because of the signed listing agreement. A deal negotiated directly with the seller without representation costs the buyer, no matter how savvy they are. Buyers just don't know what they don't know.

Dual Representation/Dual Agency

Dual representation is when a single broker represents both buyer and seller throughout the sale. Technically, the broker has a fiduciary duty to the individual they signed either a listing agreement with (seller) or an employment agreement with (buyer). The broker has an obligation to be fair and honest to the other party. It is impossible for a dual agent to fulfill a fiduciary obligation to both parties since the broker can only be hired by one or the other.

In some instances, when a speedy closing is needed and all parties of the deal fully understand the risks of dual agency, it can expedite the timeline. Yet this streamlined process can create a conflict of interest for the broker and not fully serve the buyer.

Ideally, both parties should hire their own representation when entering a commercial transaction. This removes any gray lines as to the broker's responsibilities.

Four Classic Mistakes

Billy got a smokin' deal on a 7,000-square-foot retail building for his new brewery concept—or so he thought. This was his fifth restaurant but first commercial purchase. For ten years Billy had filled his landlord's pockets, and he was ready to leave that story behind. He knew a retail purchase was the right step to build equity for himself.

Billy had bought a few homes and was confident that his residential experience was sufficient, so he felt comfortable relying on the seller's broker throughout the transaction. He identified a freestanding retail building on the corner of a high traffic intersection and put in an offer to buy. Billy rationalized that having his own representation would rock the boat and make him lose his smokin' deal. The property needed renovations, and he anticipated three months for the remodel. Billy wanted the brewery to be open before the holiday season. Everyone rushed for an early close date to start renovations. Billy built a thirty-day buffer into the construction schedule.

With no one to guide him through the potential CRE pitfalls, his naivete began to haunt him. Billy learned the city insisted on buying the corner of the property for a new traffic light, a total of 1000 square feet. This was disclosed in one of the many title documents that goes with a sale, but Billy overlooked the link. The seller had turned down two offers from the city to purchase the 1000 square feet, setting in motion an appraisal on the land and the city filing for *eminent domain*. Billy needed to hire an attorney and work with city officials to sort out this complex issue. And spend lots of money.

Industry Lingo: *Eminent domain* is the right of a government to expropriate private property for public use with payment of compensation.

Billy didn't anticipate any of this. Additionally, upon reviewing the land area the city would ultimately capture, he no longer had the amount of parking the city required.

Billy made four classic mistakes when buying his dream location:

1. He did not hire a commercial real estate buyer rep.
2. He did not utilize his *due diligence* period wisely.

3. He did not hire a commercial real estate attorney to be a third eye and go over his purchase contract or the *Schedule B* from the title company.

4. He rushed the process.

Billy now owned a property in which he would have to reduce his restaurant footprint unless the city allowed an exception to the parking requirements. More costly was an opening date two months later than anticipated.

Industry Lingo: Every purchase opportunity allows time for buyers to do homework to assure the property is fit for their business and meets their requirements. This homework period is called *due diligence* or *feasibility period*. A buyer can negotiate any amount of time to do their initial research on the property. Typically, this is thirty to ninety days depending on the circumstances.

Industry Lingo: The *Schedule B* is part of the title report itemizing "exceptions" tied to the property. These include any ownership disputes, liens, CC&R's, easements, by-laws, leases, and other items that remain of record and transfer with the property.

The Moral of the Story

Billy could have avoided some of this aggravation and cost by hiring a buyer rep. The buyer rep's job is to help with due diligence and discover possible issues in advance, which would have allowed Billy time to make an educated business decision and negotiate accordingly. In the end, Billy paid an additional $25,000 for his attorney and other industry experts. This wasn't the smokin' deal he anticipated.

Costly Mistakes Averted

So, what does buyer representation cost?

$0.00. Nothing, nada, zero, zippo. The seller pays for your buyer rep, just as when purchasing residential property.

A seller hires a listing broker to market and sell their building. This contract details the commission fee, an agreed upon percentage of the gross value of the sale price. Once there is a *fully executed purchase contract* and the transaction has closed, the seller pays the agreed upon commission to the brokerage company.

Industry Lingo: A *purchase contract* defines the purchase of real property. Some see it as the "street map" for the complete transaction.

If the listing broker is the only broker involved in the transaction, his or her firm receives the entire commission. When the buyer has representation, the gross commission is typically split fifty-fifty between the buyer rep's brokerage *house* and the listing broker's house.

Now it is clear why a listing broker is eager to assist the buyer who has no representation with the purchase. The listing broker makes twice the money.

Industry Lingo: Brokers often refer to a brokerage company as the *house*. *In-house* is when brokers refer to their commercial brokerage company.

Insider Note: Both brokers are paid a commission out of escrow once the property closes. The agreed upon percentage of the fee, usually 50 percent, goes to each commercial brokerage house. Neither broker receives 100 percent of the commission unless they are a solo designated broker. If either broker is part of a team of brokers, they must split the commission with their team. A $25,000 commission may net the lead broker as little as $5,000 based on *in-house* splits, after six months work.

Pay the Buyer Rep Direct

In some rare cases, it might be worth it to pay your buyer rep's fee directly.

Dr. Scott strategically outlined five underserved 24/7 emergency room locations in the Phoenix metropolitan area. The five locations were in outlying, newly developing areas with few building options, if any. Scott's partnership preferred to buy existing buildings and renovate within a year's time versus building from the ground up because that would take twice as long.

Dr. Scott's buyer rep located a second-generation bank on a pad already zoned for 24/7 hospital usage, an almost impossible feat. Scott and his partners were ecstatic. The property was being sold through an auction that required a specific bid process for potential buyers. Within the bidding rules it clearly spelled out that the buyer's broker would not be paid by the seller.

To secure the building, Scott's group happily paid their buyer rep a commission at the close of escrow. They knew their broker had found them the ideal property with the appropriate zoning, and they opened for business twelve months earlier than planned. It was worth every penny to support their business plan.

CHAPTER 4
Hire Your Buyer Rep

Keywords: trusted advisor, ethical, hiring, dividends, CCIM, SIOR, market knowledge, vacancy rates, absorption, analytics, negotiation skills, market value, construction costs, economics, politics, full-service gross, modified gross, triple net lease rate.

The Good, the Bad, and the Ugly

Not all buyer reps are created equal. Hiring one is akin to engaging an attorney for court or a CPA in a battle with the IRS. Experienced professionals are crucial in winning a fair shake throughout purchase contract negotiations. Consider the relationship with your buyer rep a partnership that pays dividends.

Fox in Sheep's Clothing

Abdu leased office space in a quaint, 1960s retail strip center, along with four other long-term tenants. When the owner died, he left the property to his squabbling children, who put it on the market to sell. Abdu dreamed of ownership, and now was his opportunity. Proactively, he spoke with his banker about purchasing the property. He wanted to keep the four other tenants in place and use the property as a long-term investment. The rental income from the neighboring tenants would cover his monthly mortgage, and then some. The concept of running his business rent free appealed to Abdu, and he approached the seller's listing broker for additional information.

A tenant in the strip center for over fifteen years, Abdu had paid rent like clockwork. He knew the building's history, as he had unofficially managed the property over the past five years in exchange for lower rent. The electrical panel was recently updated and more than adequate for the building. The roof needed replacing, evidenced by years of patched leaks during Arizona's monsoon season. The parking lot needed resurfacing. These deferred maintenance items were understandable, considering the property's age.

The listing broker offered to write an offer on behalf of Abdu to present to the seller. Abdu thought it a good path to follow until the listing broker insisted on presenting a full-price offer. The listing broker rationalized that his recent comparables confirmed the property value, and that sales in the area were closing at or above asking price.

Abdu smelled a fox and sought my advice. Our research concluded the listing broker's comparables were not like-kind properties built in the sixties and seventies. We strategized an offer price based on redefined comparables that an appraiser would consider. Once the property inspection report was in hand with cost estimates to replace the roof and resurface the parking lot, we negotiated a credit at the close of escrow to cover these costs. Negotiations fell in our favor when Abdu shared that the owner's kids wanted the building sold quickly so they didn't have to talk to one another again. We shifted our negotiation strategy and reduced the closing time from sixty to thirty days. Abdu's instinct to hire a buyer rep secured him a below market deal and saved him 10 percent of the list price.

Four Crucial Buyer Rep Skills:

1. Lease versus purchase assessment (necessary when deciding the next step for your business).
2. Local market knowledge and comparables (essential to negotiate the best deal).
3. Top negotiation skills (vital throughout the transaction process).
4. Ability to close the transaction. (The top three points are insignificant if title to the property never gets transferred to your name.)

Let's take a deep dive into each one:

1. Lease Versus Purchase

There is a right time to purchase your commercial building and a wrong time. Too soon, and you may grow out of your space. Too late, and you may miss an opportunity to double your retirement funds. Ask your buyer rep to prepare a lease versus purchase analysis. This helps determine your financial risk. Ask your CPA and financial planner what tax benefits building ownership offers. Take into consideration if your company needs capital for inventory, new equipment, or payroll. A high down payment for the loan may not be prudent at this juncture.

2. Local Market Knowledge

Your buyer rep must have solid market knowledge to secure a fair purchase price. Your "market" is the geographic area within which the office will be located. The buyer rep should have detailed knowledge for similar building types or be privy to this information.

Search engines are used to gather comparables and assess building information. This information is essential during the negotiation phase. Common search engines are Costar, Crexi, LoopNet, 42Floor, Property Line, and Ten-X. Regions fluctuate on which one has the most up-to-date and accurate information. Ask your potential rep which one they use and why. You may not know the advantages of one over another, but the rep's answer will tell you if he does.

Business Owner Tip: Sales are always recorded and are public information, if you know how to retrieve the data. Sales information can be verified from a broker's personal database, commercial search engine, or the county assessor's office.

When reviewing market conditions, it is beneficial for your buyer rep to review current *comps*. An informed decision helps a buyer decide to stay or move. Comps along with a lease versus purchase analysis help you decide the best direction for your company.

Industry Lingo: *Comps* is short for comparables. A broker will typically look at similar properties that sold within the last six to twelve months and assess a comparable building price. This is **not** an appraisal.

SIMPLY OWN IT!

Below is a real-life case presented to a seller, Mark, who believed his building was worth more than the price the buyer offered. The comps clearly supported a lower purchase price.

> Hi Mark—Please find attached my client's offer to purchase 10229 N 92nd. For the seller's knowledge, below is a summary of comps from the Shea corridor over the past year.
>
> I know this market intimately, and the other buildings that sold recently were in far better condition than this unit. As you are aware, 10229 N 92nd desperately needs upgrades. ☺ We believe a bank-required appraisal will support our offer price. If the seller is in agreement with the buyer's sale price, I'll draft a PSA for all parties to review. Please call with any questions. Thank you, A

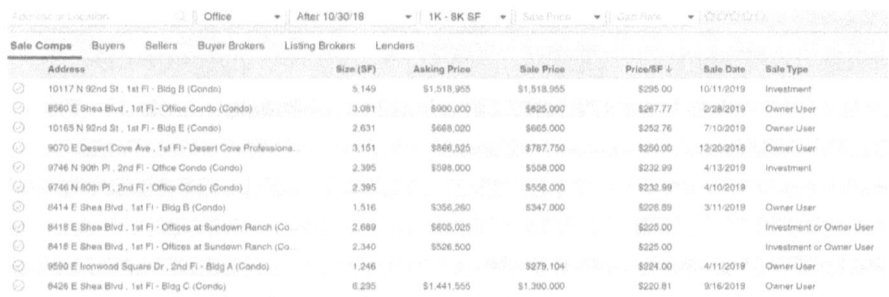

Address	Size (SF)	Asking Price	Sale Price	Price/SF ↓	Sale Date	Sale Type
10117 N 92nd St , 1st Fl - Bldg B (Condo)	5,149	$1,518,955	$1,518,955	$295.00	10/11/2019	Investment
8560 E Shea Blvd , 1st Fl - Office Condo (Condo)	3,081	$900,000	$825,000	$267.77	2/28/2019	Owner User
10165 N 92nd St , 1st Fl - Bldg E (Condo)	2,631	$688,020	$665,000	$252.76	7/10/2019	Owner User
9070 E Desert Cove Ave , 1st Fl - Desert Cove Professiona.	3,151	$866,525	$787,750	$250.00	12/20/2018	Owner User
9746 N 90th Pl , 2nd Fl - Office Condo (Condo)	2,395	$598,000	$558,000	$232.99	4/13/2019	Investment
9746 N 90th Pl , 2nd Fl - Office Condo (Condo)	2,395		$558,000	$232.99	4/10/2019	
8414 E Shea Blvd , 1st Fl - Bldg B (Condo)	1,516	$356,260	$347,000	$228.89	3/11/2019	Owner User
8418 E Shea Blvd , 1st Fl - Offices at Sundown Ranch (Co.	2,689	$605,025		$225.00		Investment or Owner User
8418 E Shea Blvd , 1st Fl - Offices at Sundown Ranch (Co.	2,340	$526,500		$225.00		Investment or Owner User
9590 E Ironwood Square Dr , 2nd Fl - Bldg A (Condo)	1,246		$279,104	$224.00	4/11/2019	Owner User
8426 E Shea Blvd , 1st Fl - Bldg C (Condo)	6,295	$1,441,555	$1,390,000	$220.81	9/16/2019	Owner User

When the email was sent, it included a detailed report of the comparables, showing that a lower price was warranted. The seller agreed to a reduced purchase price. The reduction was enough to cover the buyer's upgrades.

Third Party Appraisal

Another way to determine a building's value is to hire a certified appraiser. Your buyer rep should understand the basics of how an appraiser evaluates property values.

Three methods are used when appraising commercial real estate to determine the current value. An appraisal may cost between $2,500 and $5,000, depending on the property size, and is paid for by the buyer. This is generally done once the property is under contract and escrow has opened. All three comparisons are outlined in the appraisal. They include:

- The *Cost Approach* is the actual replacement cost of the structure and the land, taking into consideration depreciation.
- The *Market Approach* compares similar properties within a designated area and time frame. Unlike the cost approach, it does not matter what the actual cost of the property was when originally built. Rather, it relies on the fair market value of similar properties.
- The *Income Capitalization Approach* is the investment value of the property based on the revenue generated by the property.

3. Top Negotiation Skills

Buyers need strong negotiators on their side. This is where knowledge is power. The buyer rep combines knowledge of market conditions with the data gathered to negotiate the best deal possible on the buyer's behalf. Negotiations happen throughout the transaction.

Times for Key Negotiations are:

1. The initial letter of intent.

2. While reviewing the purchase contract.

3. Post appraisal report and prior to the expiration of due diligence.

4. After the building inspection report is reviewed and before the end of the due diligence period.

At any of these points, the buyer rep presents the case for a fairly written contract or a price reduction.

When you find a buyer rep with confident negotiation skills, hire him or her. Excellent negotiators:

- Listen keenly.
- Understand everyone's objectives.
- Find solutions under pressure.
- Are kind, fair, and internally strong.
- Sidestep confrontational individuals.
- Strive for win-win solutions.

4. Ability to Close

An experienced rep will need to close negotiates on behalf of the buyer at five crucial points in the sale transaction process. These moments are:

- Selling the buyer to the building owner.
- Ending the letter of intent negotiations.
- Finalizing purchase contract details.
- Wrapping up the due diligence process.
- Closing the deal.

Closing is an art often overlooked. Timing is essential. If done too quickly, it may signal desperation from the buyer and limit the ability to negotiate a lower price. If done too slowly, another buyer may usurp your position. It's similar to a conductor guiding his orchestra through the finale of a two-hour symphony. At the end, we want everyone clapping.

Opportunity Lost: Penny-wise and Pound Foolish

The Great Recession was winding down when Penny inherited money from her grandmother. She planned to invest it well. Her med spa business boomed through economic turmoil, even as property values plummeted. With the inheritance money, Penny decided to invest in her business to honor her grandmother's legacy. Buying a building was the perfect answer.

Penny sought a steal. Three low offers on three buildings later, Penny failed to secure a purchase contract. The properties were already 60 percent of their value, but Penny wanted a better deal. Savvy buyers who understood the long-term building value outbid her each time. While it was the right time for Penny to buy, and prices were low, she could not come to terms with the idea that she needed to pay "full" asking price for a good deal. As a result, Penny signed a three-year lease amendment as she monitored where the market would go. The market skyrocketed, and an acquisition fell beyond her means.

Penny needed a buyer rep to show her a different perspective on how to capitalize on a down market. A buyer rep would have provided Penny with facts to confirm that paying full price equaled a great deal.

A Couple More Considerations

Specialties: It is critically important that the broker specializes, or has significant knowledge, in acquisitions. A leasing broker doesn't know market purchase deals and vice versa. Buying an apartment complex is different than purchasing an owner/user building. Both buyers have different objectives. The buyer of a multi-family investment complex is buying an income stream. An owner/user needs the property for their specific business and is investing in themselves.

Experience: The number of transactions a broker has negotiated and closed indicates one aspect of her skill level. To access this information:

- Ask the prospective broker to describe the last few office purchase transactions she closed in your area.
- Ask what her standout moment was serving a past client.
- Spontaneously, ask what to expect to pay for a building that meets your criteria. Can she readily answer the question?
- Observe how she handles each answer. Is she confident or reluctant?

The broker's cumulative reactions and answers may indicate her comfort level when negotiating on your behalf.

Don't automatically rule out younger agents. It's not about how mature a rep is; it's about the breadth of their knowledge and experience in CRE. Older doesn't necessarily mean better.

A favorite partner of mine in his late twenties had minimal commercial experience but made up for it with book knowledge, analytics, math, and an innate talent to navigate the extensive commercial transaction process. His one shortfall was knowing when to pick up the phone and speak directly with the client, or the other side, to nudge the transaction forward.

As his mentor, there was always the moment when I'd say, "Josh, you need to make a call. Our deal is *going south*." Josh often salvaged the deal by having a conversation and finding out the client's objections. Understanding these obstacles empowered him to find a solution. Once Josh mastered the importance and timing of making the call, he was unstoppable. Today, he is invaluable to his client base.

If the broker has fewer than two years in the business, ask who their mentor is within the company, and then find out the mentor's experience level. Even a seasoned businessperson who has recently changed career paths for CRE needs a long-term mentor to navigate transactions for the first few years.

The Good

Where do you find the right buyer rep for your needs? A respected business owner often knows an experienced CRE broker and can refer you to a trusted buyer rep who assisted him with an office purchase. Your attorney, accountant, banker, or financial advisor can also be resources to find a CRE broker with a solid reputation. Or you can search online. Read prospective brokers' blogs and their online reviews. Ideally, you'll discover an informed dealmaker with an impeccable reputation in your city.

Industry leaders with a CCIM or SIOR designation are often perfect buyer reps. CCIM stands for Certified Commercial Investment Member. SIOR stands for Society for Industrial and Office Realtors. The standards and criteria for both designations are stringent; only 7 percent of commercial brokers have a CCIM and/or SIOR designation. Hiring a qualified professional with one of these two designations affirms the representative has essential transactional knowledge and meets high educational and ethical standards.

Once your options are narrowed for representation, ask each candidate broker for references. Call them.

Verify Credentials

You are really on your game, and you have made your choice of a buyer rep. Now, verify their credentials:

- Confirm their CRE broker's credentials, qualifications, and reputation.
- Validate that the buyer rep is well known within the CRE circle and aware of all potential opportunities.

- Verify the broker's reputation through LinkedIn, Instagram, Facebook, TikTok, Yelp, and Google posts and reviews.
- Check with friends and colleagues on LinkedIn who worked with the broker.

All real estate professionals must be licensed through their state to legally perform business. Confirm that your broker is registered within your state and note if any complaints have been filed with your Department of Real Estate.

The Bad and the Ugly!

You did your homework and checked off the essentials. Woe to the buyer who did not! You've heard the horror stories when the broker your friend found online pulled up late in a sporty convertible, dressed in his skinny jeans, tripping on his too-long-toed shoes, and then announced he's just learning his way around, cause he's new in town . . . Not helpful! RUN!

The golden standard means not choosing a broker who only shows you properties listed by them or their firm. Their select listings may not represent the best property for you. The broker must put your interests first. A buyer benefits by exploring all appropriate options in the marketplace, no matter what firm listed the property.

Broker Incentives

Exercise caution if the only properties presented advertise a broker commission incentive or bonus on the brochure. The broker may be considering his financial interest above yours.

Conversely, if a seller is willing to pay a buyer broker a commission bonus, it may signal a financial opportunity for the buyer. Broker bonuses are legal.

CHAPTER 5
You're Not Buying a Home

Keywords: zoning, title report, lending, ALTA survey,
Phase I report, environmental report, encumbrances,
certificate of occupancy

My parents, and probably yours, bought their home and over time accrued enough equity for a comfortable retirement. So goes ownership of commercial property.

Yet buying commercial property is not like your parent's home purchase. They are different animals in benefits and pitfalls. Throughout this chapter, you will learn step by step how to navigate buying commercial property, avoiding pitfalls to experience the greatest benefits.

There are six differences between a commercial purchase and a residential purchase:

1. Commercial Title Report: defines the legal status of property.

2. Commercial Zoning: confirms the zoning that supports your business type.

3. Commercial Lending: what will financing cost?

4. ALTA Survey: defines the boundaries of the property.

5. Environmental Survey (Phase I): is the property clean of toxic materials?

6. Certificate of Occupancy: necessary to move into your new location.

1. The Title Report

A commercial title report outlines the legal status of a specific property and related information about its ownership. It is similar to a residential title report but more involved. The title company is an impartial party in the sale process, which includes the seller, buyer, mortgage lender, and any other related party. Their primary job is to insure the property is free of encumbrances and has clear title before legal ownership passes from seller to buyer.

Encumbrances include, but are not limited to, deed restrictions, liens, easements, encroachments, and building codes. An encumbrance can lessen a property value or restrict the owner's ability to transfer title.

The title company can only transfer a clean title after certain requirements are met. Once all title issues are resolved, the title company transfers the property to the new owners.

The title company's role in closing a property will be explained further when we shadow our example buyer, Dan Campos, owner of Lifeline Insurance Group, throughout the buying process. More about differences between residential and commercial title reports can be found in step five—the title company.

2. Commercial Zoning

Commercial zoning is another area where commercial and residential acquisitions differ. While you can complete a purchase without having proper zoning for your business, the local government will not let you open your doors without it.

Zoning Example—Dr. Meca

Dr. Meca identified a secondary community in need of a micro hospital. His goal was to buy a freestanding building large enough for a 24/7 acute care facility and an urgent care center, about 10,000 square feet with room to expand. Locating a *second-generation building* meant he would be open for business within six to nine months, yet there were few options to consider. After scouring the targeted area, no building could be found with the right zoning.

Industry Lingo: *second-generation building* or secondary space refers to a previously occupied building or a commercial condo that becomes available for sale.

Dr. Meca shifted directions. A micro hospital with its specific architectural needs turned out to be more cost effective to build from the ground up. Land became the primary focus, even though it extended Dr. Meca's ideal timeline of six months by another year.

The quintessential location presented itself near a major intersection. An exploratory meeting with town officials affirmed that a 24/7 micro hospital could be built on the parcel. The town, excited for a community hospital, guesstimated Dr. Meca's opening date within twelve months from the initial meet and greet if his development team double timed the process.

Four weeks into the due diligence process, the time when a buyer does their homework to confirm the property works for them and financing is secured, the town advised Dr. Meca the hospital needed a special use permit to be open 24/7. This new information meant that Dr Meca's group would need a public hearing. This process involved neighborhood input, meetings, and approval from the town council. The doctor had no guarantee the project would be approved at the end of the public outreach and council vote. This new request from the town cost the doctor additional money and increased his timeline from one year to eighteen to twenty-four months.

Business Owner Tip: When you want to open a business quickly, an existing building is often less costly and timelier. Finding land to build could mean delays and other complications.

Even with 100 percent support from town council members, the mayor, and most citizens, a few grumbling *NIMBY* neighbors held the project up through public appeal another three months. This almost cost the doctor his financing, which was tied to a groundbreaking date to start construction.

Industry Lingo: *NIMBY* is an acronym for "not in my backyard."

3. Not Your Mother's Home Loan

The most common pitfall commercial property buyers make is to equate the commercial loan process with residential financing. This is like comparing a dog to a cat. They are different species. The two types of loans differ drastically, from prequalification to closing. The differences between a commercial loan and a residential loan are discussed in detail under step six—the lender and due diligence.

$$$ Saving Tip: Don't assume your primary banker offers the best commercial lending terms. Shop around to compare terms. Lenders are competitive, and they offer different loan packages and incentives. Do your homework. It is like buying a car; you shop around until you get the best deal.

It's always good to know if you are getting fair terms from your lender. Sam planned to purchase a freestanding building for her physician's office. She requested loan terms from three lenders. One lender's initial proposal offered a fixed interest rate of 6.25 percent interest for fifteen years. Another proposal came in at a fixed 5.29 percent for fifteen years, and the third offered a special fixed rate of 3.9 percent for ten years. This provided Sam some bargaining power when choosing her lender.

Ideally, Sam wanted a fifteen-year fixed rate. When lender number three, a local bank, offered Sam a 4.2 percent loan at fifteen years fixed, she accepted. The bank's one condition was for Sam to move her business banking to their branch.

4. Commercial Real Estate Only: The ALTA Survey

The title company or lender may require a current *ALTA survey* (American Land Title Association) on the property before a clear title will be insured for the new owner. While the title company requires the ALTA survey, the lender orders it. The survey may cost the buyer as much as $3,000 depending on the property type and size. This cost can be rolled into your loan.

Industry Lingo: *ALTA survey* **(American Land Title Association)**

The ALTA survey outlines the property boundaries, diagrams the location of improvements on the property (such as structures, fences, utility lines, roads, etc.), and includes all easements. The survey must be completed by a registered, licensed surveyor.

$$$ Saving Tip: Depending on when the last ALTA survey was issued, you can request the original survey company update the report. This may save you up to 50 percent of the survey cost.

When a buyer pays cash for a property, an ALTA survey is not required. It is recommended, however, especially on older properties. ALTA surveys can help uncover unexpected surprises.

Boundaries and lot lines often create interesting scenarios. Greg's desire to purchase involved more than he bargained for. The thirty-year-old building sat on a split lot and had been sold that way at least two previous times.

Greg's new 15,000-square-foot building supported his company's growth, so he signed a contract at $2,250,000. During the forty-five-day due diligence period, Schedule B documents from the title company revealed the property shared a water meter with the neighboring building. An ALTA survey confirmed the discovery. Further discoveries uncovered that the parcel had never been legally separated, even though the two buildings were recorded as separate tax parcels. This was quite unusual and put the city in the driver's seat. Before the city would allow the new buyer permits for improvements, the property needed separate water meters and a lot split.

$$$ Saving Tip: Generally, the buyer should seek an attorney to review Schedule B exceptions and write up any objections for the title company to consider. It pays off over the long term.

The big question is: who pays for the lot split? It is negotiable, and in this case, the seller ultimately conceded to the financial burden because he couldn't sell the property any other way.

Nine months later, two commercial real estate attorneys, numerous city officials, two building owners, and a potential buyer were still working on the city's lot split requirement. The property's value had increased 10 percent. The sellers refused to extend the due diligence period unless Greg paid a higher price for the building.

Greg's Decision

Greg had two choices: cancel the purchase or continue knowing he'd have to pay more. Buying commercial property always entails financial risk. A buyer pays dearly during the due diligence phase of the purchase to make an informed decision. The key is to invest wisely, making sure all *feasibility* studies are completed prior to the expiration of the buyer's due diligence period. If the buyer decides to cancel after the due diligence timeframe expires, earnest monies are usually forfeited to the seller.

Greg decided to take his losses and run. After weighing the pros and cons, Greg chose to cancel escrow and request the return of his $100,000 earnest money. Greg had to invest $15,000 to discover the property would cost substantially more to retrofit. He tallied the cost and decided to find a new opportunity.

What If Greg Decided to Buy?

Let's explore Greg's decision to cancel escrow and take the $15,000 hit. The buyer wanted an additional $250,000 to purchase the building, increasing the purchase price to $2,500,000. Additionally, Greg's $100,000 would become non-refundable if he continued with the purchase. That meant if Greg canceled escrow later, the $100,000 earnest monies would be legally surrendered to the seller. As Greg discovered, this scenario financially stretched him to the limit.

The legal spider web to separate the two lots would take another six months. This meant Greg would incur a 150 percent *holdover rent* fee, spelled out in most leases, on his current location. Greg's monthly rent was $8,000 a month. The holdover cost would add $4,000 more in rent per month while Greg's attorney sorted out the lot split.

Industry Lingo: *Holdover rent* is 50–100 percent higher than what a buyer is currently paying monthly. This amount is negotiated prior to signing your lease. The rent increase starts upon the lease expiration date, and all other terms of the lease remain in effect. If possible, a buyer wants to avoid a holdover fee. But it is better than being evicted prematurely.

Business Owner Tip: Don't assume your holdover clause is automatically enforceable. Most leases require that activation of a holdover clause be agreed to in writing by landlord and buyer in advance of the lease termination date.

DO THE MATH – Greg's New 15,000 SF building:

Original price:	$2,250,000
Architectural cost ($4 SF):	$ 60,000
Buildout cost ($30 SF):	$ 450,000
Greg's anticipated total building cost:	**$2,760,000**
Nine months later, Greg's additional costs to continue with the lot split:	$ 250,000
Higher building price:	
Higher loan payment ($1,500 mo. over 25 years):	$ 450,000
Holdover rental cost ($4,000 for 6 months):	$ 24,000
Subtotal:	**$ 724,000**
Total new building acquisition cost:	**$3,484,000**

Greg's new building increased 26 percent from his earlier financial calculations. Moving forward with the additional expenditures was prudent only if Greg could justify the increased cost.

5. *Environmental Report:* Commercial Only

Another aspect of buying commercial versus residential property is that a lender and the title company may require an *environmental report* on the property, also known as a Phase I. The Phase I is an explorative report that digs into the property's history, along with a site visit to determine if further investigation is required. The report assesses the likelihood of impurities on site, such as lead, oil, and/or toxic chemicals. If any contaminant is found, a Phase II report will be ordered for additional information. A Phase III report is ordered when the property needs to be professionally remediated to EPA standards. This can be costly and should be the seller's cost, presuming the seller made the mess.

Industry Lingo: An *environmental report* is an investigation on commercial property to discover whether there are any dangerous contaminants in the soil or groundwater that could pose a threat to the environment and/or human health. Industrial, manufacturing, even gas stations and auto repair shops, could be subject to these requirements.

In residential language, an environmental report might be considered an in-depth Sellers Property Disclosure Statement (SPDS).

Environmental Report—Harold's Story

Harold owned a landscape business. He objected when his lender ordered a Phase I report prior to closing on his new building.

"Why do I need to pay $2,500 for a Phase I report when the property is spotless inside and out? It isn't even in a Super Fund area of town."

The Phase I report revealed lead in the soil. A contractor who owned the property in the 1960s had cleaned lead-based paint sprayers on site. The contamination remediation, or clean-up, cost the seller over $15,000. Again, this is a requirement the lender and title company need for a clean title transfer, so it behooved the seller to pay the cost. Yes, Harold was glad the lender required a Phase I report. He saved $15,000 and received a clear property title and documentation of the environmental remediation for future buyers.

$$$ Saving Tip: Office condos may not require a full environmental report. Often the lender is content with an environmental questionnaire filled out by the seller. This saves the buyer time and money.

Business Owner Tip: Whether you finance or pay cash, it is good practice to obtain a new or updated ALTA survey and environmental report. The buyer pays for this report because the lender requires it and wants to select the party who generates the findings.

6. Yet Another Difference: Certificate of Occupancy and Zoning

Prior to occupying a commercial building, most municipalities require a *Certificate of Occupancy (C of O)*.

Industry Lingo: A *Certificate of Occupancy (C of O)* is a document issued by a local government agency that confirms a building's legal use (i.e., commercial, retail, or industrial) is suitable for occupancy and ensures the structure complies with all building codes.

To receive a C of O, the following items need to meet local and federal government regulations: (make like other bullet points)

✓ The property is zoned for the business use.

✓ The building meets city building codes and is suitable for occupancy.

✓ Adequate parking is available for employees and clients.

✓ There is safe ingress and egress to the building.

✓ The building meets ADA (Americans with Disabilities Act) requirements.

✓ There may be other requirements based on where your business is located.

Different business types require specific zoning. A shop owner usually needs retail zoning, whereas a general office user requires office zoning, and a warehouse user is limited to industrial zoned sites. Some businesses, such as medical users, can practice in more than one zoning category. Zoning ordinances are critical and vary from city to city. Your broker can recommend a zoning attorney to interpret zoning ordinances and guide clients through the rezoning process. Proactively check with your local municipality to verify the zoning code requirements for your type of business use before falling in love with a property. This is public knowledge and generally can be found on a municipal website. For example, to find out zoning for a client, I search Google for "Scottsdale zoning ordinance." Or you can go directly to your city's website.

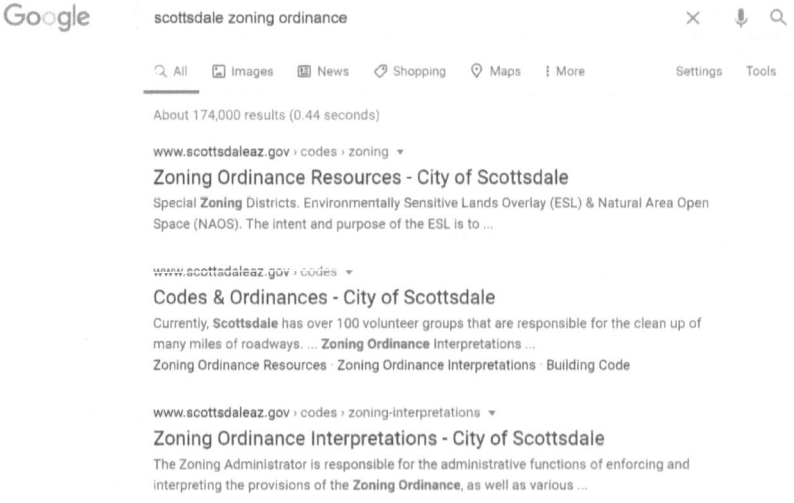

Once I'm on the website, I pull up the zoning ordinance and search the parcel's designated zoning to see if it supports my client's business use. For one client, we needed to verify that C-4 would support auto sales. A search confirmed it did. As a property owner, you also want to verify zoning for yourself.

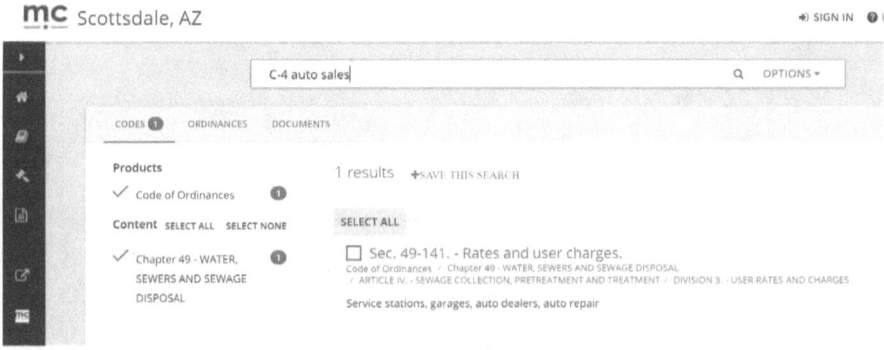

Business Owner Tip: Rezoning is time consuming and costly. It requires neighborhood involvement and city approval. Ensuring the community supports your vision can take more than a year. To increase the likelihood of winning this complex government process, hire a local zoning attorney.

Business Owner Tip: Check with the title company about purchasing additional title insurance for specific endorsements, such as zoning. This ensures that if there's a zoning challenge down the road, the title company takes on the challenge at their cost.

There is one more important aspect to explore before jumping into the practical step-by-step approach to buying commercial real estate, and that is market conditions.

CHAPTER 6

Market Conditions, Key to Negotiations

Keywords: seller's market, buyer's market, negotiations

Market Definition

Market conditions are a combination of varying economic factors. They influence how much a buyer is willing to pay for a building and what a seller can justify charging. Key elements that affect market conditions include:

- Interest rates and lender terms.
- Global and local economic trends, such as the financial crises in 2008 and 2020.
- Demographic shifts, such as how Millennials differ from Baby Boomers in their wants, needs, and requirements in their community.
- Disappearing small businesses.

- Urbanization trends such as technology, higher density, self-driving cars, and online retail outlets like Amazon.
- Politics and government policies.
- Credit constraints.
- Energy supply or lack thereof.
- Emerging virtual economies such as Uber, Airbnb, Divvy, cooperative or at-home work environments, blockchain, and crowdfunding.
- Pandemic.
- Supply chain interruptions.

It's All in a Day

Market conditions are a NEED TO KNOW for all business owners. Changing market conditions creep up on the public overnight, seemingly taking the businessperson by surprise. For the buyer, it can be the difference between negotiating your purchase contract in a seller's market when properties are scarce, or a buyer's market when building supplies are plentiful.

In a buyer's market there is an abundance of inventory for sale, generally spurred on by economic changes locally and nationally. During these times, a building owner might be in a jam with a depressed economy and business disruption. Not able to make mortgage payments, he might need a fire sale. If there is an abundance of similar product on the market, a seller's negotiation power is decreased.

In a seller's market, property inventory is low, and sale prices are less flexible. This is the law of supply and demand. Negotiations are in the seller's favor, and one can anticipate a bidding war with more than one buyer. As the market condition pendulum shifts, both parties adjust accordingly.

Bryan's Story—Timing and Patience

Bryan's aftermarket boat customization business needed 13,000 square feet for indoor repairs and a large outside yard for storage. These specifications are akin to finding a needle in a haystack, requiring patience until "that" property comes on the market. Any compromise on the yard meant Bryan's business would suffer.

As Bryan's rep, I stayed in close touch and regularly informed him of sold properties in his desired area so that when the right property availed itself, Bryan would be abreast of market conditions and be able to act quickly and intelligently.

Bryan positioned himself financially so that when the timing was right, he knew how to secure a property. After a year of searching and door knocking, we found the perfect warehouse space with a fenced-in yard. The owner wanted to retire. We offered a purchase price slightly over market value and secured the sale before it had a chance to go to market. The timing? The pendulum leaned toward the beginning of a seller's market.

His patience and investment in current market knowledge netted Bryan the ideal property. Five years later he needed a larger building. The market climbed in Bryan's favor, and he sold the warehouse for a record price. It was a full-on seller's market by then.

The World Stops

Historically sellers' and buyers' markets can be predicted by economists quite reliably. Yet when COVID-19 struck, America's bull economy avalanched into a bear market. Coronavirus changed the world overnight and brought crucial industries to their knees. Industries such as financing, tourism, transportation, entertainment, food industries, and small businesses of all types were in uncharted waters.

In a split second, a hot seller's market screeched to a halt. No one wanted a fire sale, unless in dire straits, and no one could buy without cash. Buyers and tenants were in the driver seat again, yet most businesses froze in time, unable to capitalize on this unprecedented opportunity.

Economic conditions are a science. Regional markets are affected differently by economic changes. Some areas thrive, some plod along, and others decline. In the case of COVID-19, all markets crashed simultaneously. A first for the world to experience.

Market Cycles Influence Negotiations

How your buyer rep negotiates with a seller varies depending on the market cycle. This table highlights the ins and outs of market conditions from a buyer and a seller perspective.

Reasons a Buyer Market Exists	Reasons a Sellers Market Exists
Abundant supply and low demand	Lack of supply and high demand
Stagnant or struggling economy	Stimulated economy
Overbuilt market	Underbuilt market
High vacancy in building types	Low vacancy in building types
Slow product absorption	Rapid product absorption

Dr. Singh's Story—Patience Pays Off

Dr. Singh's oncology business thrived in a 6,000-square-foot office condo at the back of a 120,000-square-foot office project. He needed more space to expand his business and wanted to add an imaging center for his patient's convenience. The building next door was the ideal expansion location. Its 11,000 square feet shell had been vacant for years. We tracked down the owner and wrote an aggressive purchase offer. The owner said no and refused to counter. He/she sat on the building for another two years, paying about $55,000 a year in HOA fees and property taxes. After four years the owner had sunk $220,000 into the building and received only a tax deduction.

When the owner finally put the property on the market a half a year later, Dr. Singh bought it for less than his original offer. The market by then favored a lower price, the seller needed to sell, and Dr. Singh bought the property for a song.

Luke's Story—Demand in a Seller's Market

Property owners like to time their exit during a seller's market. Luke was moving out of state and knew the value of his *flex warehouse* in north Scottsdale had escalated. He didn't know by how much until his listing went live.

Industry Lingo: A *flex warehouse* is a combination of warehouse space and office space. Generally, flex properties are converted warehouse spaces that are 100 percent air-conditioned and have a rollup door.

Luke Printing's flex building was listed for $1,265,000 on Monday. Within thirty-six hours, four offers were received. All were for cash, and two were at the full asking price. The seller's broker asked each participant for a best and final offer. Luke's broker presented him with an analysis of the four offers:

Name	Dental Lab	Rattler Concrete	SEOE	Lemon Trees
Price	$1,285,000	$1,265,000	$1,285,000	$1,286,000
Cash	Yes	Yes	yes	Yes
Earnest monies	$45,000	$50,000	$50 000 total	$50,000
Immediate Nonrefundable	No	no	$15,000.00	No
Due diligence period	15 days	15 days	21 days	20 days
Closing Period	15 days	15 days	7 days	10 days

Three of the best and final offers came back $20,000 over the asking price. How was this possible? There were no other properties this size in the area. Market conditions were in favor of the seller. Swift marketing and prompt responses to potential buyers created a bidding war, where the seller cashed out on his building in thirty days when the average sale time was sixty.

The seller accepted the offer from the party who put up $15,000 nonrefundable from day one.

When to Buy?—Sam's International Gymnastics

Sam's International Gymnastics lease was set to expire in a year. Over the past ten years, the business had stabilized. In year one, Sam leased 5,000 square feet and jumped up to 10,000 square feet in year three. She now leased 15,000 square feet, paying $18,000 a month in rent. Sams nonresponsive landlord guaranteed Sam she would have a rent increase at the end of the year.

SIMPLY OWN IT!

Sam's New Year's resolution was to be her own landlord. The market was on fire, and buildings were scarce in her desired area of town. The few buildings she found online for sale are priced high and would require significant buyer improvements. Sam doubted she could actualize her dream. She wisely dialed her commercial buyer rep.

Fortunately for Sam, interest rates were at an all-time low. When her buyer rep did the math, she found that a monthly mortgage would be equal to or less than what Sam was currently paying for rent.

What will the monthly mortgage payment be for Sam to buy a building? It depends on interest rates, building price, and how much of a down payment she can afford. Let's make some assumptions.

Do the Math:

Building cost: 15,000 SF x $140 per SF = 2,100,000

10% Down payment: (SBA financing): $210,000

Loan amount: $1,890,000

Interest amount: 5.5%

Amortized over: 25 years

Monthly loan payment: $11,600

Plus, building maintenance estimated at $3 SF: $3,750 monthly

Total equivalent monthly payment to buy is: $15,350

Sam's current monthly lease payment: $18,000

As a building owner, Sam would save $2,650 every month over her rental payment.

That equates to $31,800 each year or over **$318,000 in ten years' time**.

Additionally, Sam would receive tax benefits and building appreciation. To purchase a building, the numbers are in Sam's favor.

In Theory

While in theory, buying sounds like the perfect solution for Sam, there was much more to consider. Could she qualify for the loan, and did she have enough liquidity for the down payment?

In fact, Sam did qualify for a loan. Yet her dream still might not come true. Her requirement was so specific—high ceilings and large open spaces without support beams—that she may not be able to find a building due to low market inventory.

Building a custom gymnasium was not an option for Sam because of the time required to build, up to twenty-four months, and Sam only had twelve months remaining on her lease. Additionally, construction costs were high. In other words, a build-to-suit for Sam would cost dramatically more than finding a second-generation building to remodel, which would cut time and cost.

Even with a dream of ownership, it may be out of reach because of market conditions. In Sam's case, there was a happy ending. She found a building that met her primary requirements: location, clear height, and well-placed support beams. She had to compromise on size. The building was 3,000 square feet larger than she thought she needed, so she leased it out to a synergistic business, a yoga studio, and used the income to offset her higher mortgage payment.

A qualified buyer rep will advise you on whether it is a seller's market or a buyer's market. Experienced brokers who have lived through the ebb and flow of a few decades can accurately predict which way the pendulum points for purchase prices. Listening to their advice will be remunerative.

PART II

The Nine-Step Process

STEP ONE
Strategic Plan, the Power of Preparation

Keywords: buying parameters, lease versus purchase, when to buy, shell space, second generation space, digital marketing

Timeframe: *one to two weeks*

Meet Lifeline Insurance

Lifeline Insurance experienced tremendous growth by using a long-term marketing strategy. Owner Dan Campos' new branding campaign wrapped digital marketing, SEO stealth, and a strong social media presence together with regular Google, Yelp, and positive online client reviews. The magic soup meant business escalated tenfold.

Explosive Growth

Dan knows expansion is in his future. His strategy includes property ownership and accruing building equity until he sells his company.

Dan seeks buyer representation from Amanda, a commercial real estate veteran. Their conversation opens behind a counter at his crowded office. Formalities are exchanged, then Dan begins, "I own this office condo and enjoy the benefits of ownership, especially being my own landlord."

He ushers Amanda to his tidy office. "As you saw when you came in, my employees are on top of one another, and I need to do something. My business doubled in the last two years, and I don't want to make the same mistake I made with this place. I bought too small and now my business growth is limited to the size of the office. I'm not sure ownership is the right approach for the next phase of my business."

They settle in, and Amanda pulls out a notepad to jot down notes. "That's a legitimate concern. Tell me more about your future business plans, such as where do you see yourself in five, even ten years, and about your exit strategy."

"I need twice the space I have here, which is about 5,000 square feet, and ideally, I'd like to own but I'm not sure it's time. Landlords . . ." Dan shakes his head. "Well, I'll leave it at that. I see my business stabilizing in five years and possibly opening another branch in the West Valley."

"Ownership is the easiest way to control your financial future. Why do you think leasing might be better?"

Dan replies, "Two reasons. First, I anticipate doubling again in a short time. I don't want to buy and outgrow the next building. Second, I might need my spare capital for growth. And third, I'm not super excited to buy in a seller's market unless you can find me a deal I can live with. So, that's my quandary." Dan shifts in his chair.

Step By Step

Amanda takes the cue. "Let's break your decision down step by step. You're correct, we are in a seller's market. Inventory is extremely low. I'm exploring outside of our standard databases to fulfill other client's requirements in this area, and we're having success. Until we explore all options, I suggest we look at reasons for you to buy now versus lease."

Dan taps his pen. "Such as . . ."

"First, interest rates are so low—close to 4 percent—and lenders are aggressively financing owner/user properties. Your mortgage obligation will remain constant, while a lease increases annually. Second, if we can find you a second-generation office building, the price you pay will be less than building from the ground up."

"I was going to ask you about buying land and putting up a structure. I'm not sure I can wait for the construction timeline, but I'm open to the idea." It is clear Dan has been considering the next best real estate step for his expanding company.

"Ok, let's talk about building from the ground up." Amanda takes her retro calculator from her handbag and starts tapping. "Construction costs have escalated in the past ten years—almost doubled. To build from scratch, I suspect you'd need to budget $425 per square foot, which includes the land. If we find you the right building, it'll cost around $350 per square foot. A second generation 10,000-square-foot office will be about $750,000 less than a new building. If you're patient, we'll probably find the ideal site within a year versus the two years to build."

Amanda lets the numbers sink in.

"That's a considerable difference. For my business to grow, I need to relocate sooner than two years. It might be best for me to consider a short-term lease. What does the leasing environment look like?"

"It's a less competitive market than buying a building, that's for sure. We'll prepare a simple lease versus purchase analysis to run by your CPA and/or financial planner. We'll explore both options, lease and purchase, for you to make an educated decision. Sometimes the numbers speak for themselves."

Steps to Analyze This Question: *"Is a purchase right for me now?"*

1. Review where your business is today and where you envision it in two, five, and ten years.

2. Examine tax benefits.

3. Analyze a market lease versus purchase spreadsheet with your buyer rep, financial planner, and CPA. Minimally, enter these factors into the formula:

   a. Size of the property.

   b. Current lease rates.

   c. Lease incentives such as rent abatement, landlord buyer improvement contribution, moving allowance, free covered parking, etc.

   d. Current property values.

   e. Buyer improvement costs to the building provided by a contractor.

   f. Interest rate, amortization term, and down payment.

4. Compare the initial cost of leasing, first and last month's rent, versus 10 to 20 percent down to purchase.

5. Explore inventory options in the marketplace.

6. Discuss lending options with multiple lenders.

Amanda says, "A thought just occurred to me, with your strong online success, will moving into a different zip code affect the business that is driven from online marketing? When I rebranded, my online leads dropped for about six months."

The Follow Up

Dan follows up the next day. His ideal solution is a 10,000-square-foot building in the same zip code he is currently in. His marketing guru confirmed that he needs to remain in Gilbert to maintain his strong online business presence. This can be a second-generation building or a *shell building*. The backup plan, due to lack of inventory and a seller's market, is for Dan to stay in his current location for his digital marketing and open a second office in an area with future growth. Dan will entertain buying a piece of land to build an office.

Industry Lingo: A *shell building* is the minimum enclosure of a building, including foundation, floors, structural framework, roof coverings, exterior walls and exterior doors and windows, basic fire sprinkler systems, underground electrical power stubs, plumbing system stubs, parking lots, and landscaping. Buyer improvements' design and buildout are at the expense of the new owner.

Dan's Buying Parameters—Questions and Answers

Top-notch buyer reps hone your property parameters and manage the search process. This is a chart Amanda uses for Dan to pinpoint his search parameters.

Andrea Davis

CRITERIA	QUESTION	ANSWER
Location	Where is your ideal location?	Gilbert in zip code 85233 because of digital marketing.
Near Amenities	Is it important to have restaurants, medical professionals, shopping amenities, etc. near by?	YES
Parking	How many spaces?	4 per 1,000 square feet of building.
Access	Do you need or want easy access?	YES
Freeway Access	Is freeway access necessary?	Not necessary – clients seldom come to the office.
Signage	How important is signage?	Not necessary as online branding is key yet would like for resale purposes.
High Visibility	Does your business require high visibility?	No but helps with resale value.

PROPERTY	QUESTION	ANSWER
Building Size	How many square feet do you need?	10,000 SF.
Zoning	What zoning is required for your type of business? Office, retail, industrial?	Office or retail.
Building Style	Do you prefer a fee simple property or an office condo?	Any style.
New or Second Generation	Do you want a new building or one that may need renovation?	Will consider all options.

TIMING	QUESTION	ANSWER
Move-in Date	When does your lease expire?	Goal is to relocate within 6-12 months. No lease.
Timing Flexibility	Can you holdover or go month to month at your current location if move-in is delayed?	Read your lease and check if you have an 'hold over' clause and how much it is.
Renovation	What is the estimate time for renovations?	6 months – more if there are supply chain issues.
Build-to Suit	Do you have 18-24 months to build from the ground up?	Last choice unless you have flexibility and time.

FINANCING	QUESTION	ANSWER
Debt	What can you afford?	Lender says Joe can finance up to $3 million.
Budget Estimate	Common area maintenance, property taxes, insurance, HVAC	This is in addition to the monthly mortgage payment.
Down Payment Range	How much can you put down?	Up to $300,000

STEP TWO
Identify Potential Properties

Keywords: property search, discovery phase, keep an open mind, Class A, Class B, Class C, summarize, short-list

Timeline: one to five days for buyer rep to search and verify properties with the buyer

Step one defined search parameters for your property. Step two narrows the search and sets up the tour. Here we delve into the discovery phase to understand the building purchase requirement. Both buyer and buyer's rep explore available building options within a client's designated budget, location, and timeframe.

The Initial Search

Plan as you might, a business owner never knows when they will find that perfect fit for their company. Some buyers search and search to find the perfect place, while others stumble upon the property by accident.

Fred wanted to tour every building on the market within a broad geographic area before deciding on the perfect one, so he explored all possible options for a year before making an offer. He found the perfect property, so he didn't have to make a panic decision. The building he selected met all his criteria and successfully supported the next phase of his business.

Tyson, on the other hand, knew exactly where he wanted to locate his mortgage company. He was set on a nonconventional warehouse condo complex near his home. After two years of patience, an owner agreed to sell. For Tyson, it was worth the wait. His wife liked the new office because Tyson designed the space to store all his motorized toys, and her car finally fit in the home garage.

Each business has unique criteria, such as proximity to freeways or airports, physical attributes of the building, and even synergy with surrounding businesses. Buyers' parameters for price, size, and location are entered into a commercial property database.

Below is a search example from Costar, a common search provider similar to the residential MLS search engine and known by most commercial real estate professionals. The sample includes a map of property choices with a brief description, including location and square footage.

For Sale Map & List Report

Records	Avg. Cap Rate	Avg. Price/SF	Avg. Vacancy
4	**6.6%**	**$404**	**31.7%**

FOR SALE LOCATIONS

Map data ©2021

FOR SALE SUMMARY STATISTICS

Sales Attributes	Low	Average	Median	High
Sale Price	$2,700,000	$5,342,500	$3,010,000	$12,650,000
Price/SF	$241	$405	$267	$843
Cap Rate	6.1%	6.6%	6.6%	7.1%
Days on Market	105	205	157	400

Property Attributes	Low	Average	Median	High
Building SF	10,402	12,185	11,669	15,000
Floors	1	1	1	2
Typical Floor	5,613	9,375	10,402	12,111
Vacancy Rate	0%	31.7%	13.4%	100%
Year Built	1984	1989	1985	1999

	Property					Sale			
Property Name - Address	Type	Yr Built	Size	Vacancy	Price	Price/Area	Cap Rate	Days on Market
1 Lou Malnati's & The... 2 Properties Portfolio	Retail & Office	-	15,000 SF	0%	$12,650,000	$843/SF	6.1%	105
2 Bldg 6 8960 E Raintree Dr Scottsdale, AZ 85260 ★★★★★	Office	1999	12,111 SF	0%	$3,270,000	$270/SF	-	147
3 Via Linda Prof Plaza 9188 E San Salvador Dr Scottsdale, AZ 85258 ★★★★★	Medical	1985	11,226 SF	26.7%	$2,700,000	$241/SF	7.1%	166
4 5620 E Bell Rd Scottsdale, AZ 85254 ★★★★★	Medical	1984	10,402 SF	100%	$2,750,000	$264/SF	-	400

85

Once one or more properties are identified for further study, additional information is presented for the buyer to review. Often this overview is accompanied by the property brochures with specific details. This Costar example shows building details on the selected property options.

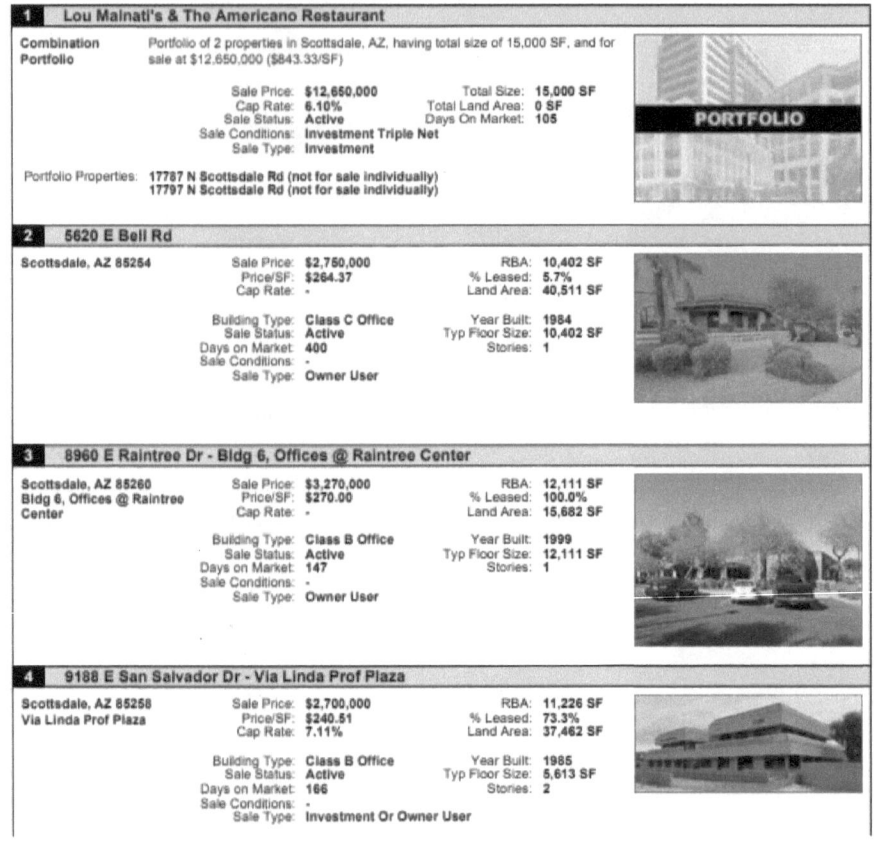

An initial search often reveals more properties than can be toured in a reasonable amount of time. For efficiency, the buyer and rep narrow down a few top properties for a preliminary review. Buyers often want to drive by the properties on their own to narrow the list. A buyer rep assists the buyer in organizing the process.

Enter Stage Left: The Discovery Phase

The search is on! Buyer reps do their best to narrow down targeted options for buyers, but it's not a perfect science. Be realistic. Odds are the ideal property doesn't appear on an initial tour. Expect the unexpected on the first look. A buyer's vision of their dream building is seldom clear until they see firsthand what's available. Sometimes what the buyer wants isn't obtainable when the search begins. A buyer and their rep may have to think outside the box for a property to fit their vision.

Diane's clinical psychology client base needed ADA facilities within an office. Sensitive to her patients' needs, Diane set her No. 1 search parameter as a single-story building. After six months of searching and no results, her broker suggested a two-story property in a quaint commercial neighborhood close to Diane's home. Reluctantly, Diane agreed to tour the property, even though she was adamantly opposed to a two-story property with stairs and no elevator. Despite herself, she liked it. The 2,000 SF office was bright and cheery, just what her clients needed, and well within her budget. She just needed to come up with a clever way to meet ADA requirements for her practice.

Her buyer rep noted the stairway was wider than normal and suggested exploring a chair lift to accommodate her handicapped patients. The next day a representative from the stair lift company met them onsite and determined it was a viable option. Diane wrote an offer that day and never looked back.

If the first tour doesn't produce acceptable options, no worries! A competant buyer rep continues a property search until the right property is discovered.

You Know What You Want . . . Until You Don't

Another client was convinced she needed a *Class A*, top-notch, freestanding office building for branding and a high-end client base. That was until she toured a freestanding *Class B* office condo with a custom-designed interior.

The buyer was surprised to find the Class B office condo had a classier interior and a distinctive presence over Class A office buildings. The Class B property cost less per square foot, allowed building signage, and had extensive patron parking. The client purchased the Class B office building and was thrilled that she could move into the spotless property immediately upon closing.

Industry Lingo:

- *Class A* office buildings are state-of-the art and offer current cultural trends. They are in a superior location and generally a newer property. Class A buildings are the most expensive to purchase.
- *Class B* office buildings are well-kept older properties, generally in strong locations. Often these buildings are targeted by investors for renovation.
- *Class C* properties are older buildings in less desirable areas, lacking in quality finishes, and they may be in need of maintenance. Sale prices are lower.

$$$ Saving Tip: If you want a high-end office, don't rule out Class B office space. It often costs less than Class A office space and it doesn't mean the building is out-of-date or lacking character.

Every client has their own individual wish list for a property. A digital consulting firm put the need for visibilty high on their initial priority list, even though the bulk of the firm's business came from social media and the web. While on tour, the buyer's rep ascertained the company needed easy access for clients coming to the office. Their current office was buried deep within a large multi-building office complex and difficult to find.

$$$ Saving Tip: Understand where your clients commute from and what their expectations are for your business's appearance before starting your search. If your company doesn't need visibility in a trendy area of town, don't pay for it.

It wasn't long until the firm found a quality office building at a well-known but lightly traveled intersection. Instead of paying an exorbitant price for a building with high visibility, they found a modern office conveniently located, with building signage and a moderate price tag. The company shifted the dollars it saved with a lower mortgage payment into additional social media marketing.

Property Short-List Guide for Initial Tour

Ideally, a short list of properties to tour includes:
- Building name and location.
- Building size and age.
- Property size and zoning.
- Parking ratio.
- Asking price.
- Expenses (property taxes, HOA fees, or maintenance costs).
- If there is a tenant in place, rental income.

Once the tour is agreed upon, the buyer rep coordinates with the sellers' brokers. Most sellers want their representative on location when an office space is toured to answer buyer questions immediately. A seller's rep highlights building attributes the buyer rep may not be aware of.

An exceptional buyer rep compiles a customized summary that includes a map of the properties, a time schedule, brochures, and floor plans for each suite on the tour. This booklet is perfect for taking notes during a tour. Below is an example of a property tour overview. In this instance, the buyer will consider buildings with tenants as part of the purchase. The spreadsheet includes rental income on two property options. Some buyers like additional rental income when purchasing a property for their business.

Property				
Address	8937 E Bell	9170 E Bahia	9903 E Bell	7363 E Adobe
Type	Office	Flex	Office	Warehouse
Zoning	C-3 PCD	I-1 light industrial		C-4
Size	8,520	5,251	6,512	7,047
Covered Parking	8	0 / warehouse space	6	yes?
Stories	2	1+ mezzanine	1	1+ mezzanine
Asking	$2,343,000.00	$1,564,069.00	$1,625,000.00	$1,650,000.00
Price SF	$275.00	$297.86	$249.54	$234.14
ANNUAL Expenses				
POA annual	$21,348.96	$5,773.44	$15,628.80	$9,444.00
Property Taxes	$7,188.00	$5,796.72	$11,738.10	$10,456.50
Electric	$21,300.00	$11,814.75	$8,670.46	$7,098.65
Total	$49,836.96	$23,384.91	$36,037.36	$26,999.15
HOA & Taxes SF	$5.85	$4.45	$5.53	$3.83
INCOME				
Tenant 1	Yes - Mask - 5 yr	No	Firedrum - 2 yr	No
Annaul NOI	$59,640.00	$0.00	$20,640.00	$0.00
Tenant 2	No	No	Bank 12/20	No
Annual NOI	$0.00	$0.00	$32,746.50	$0.00
TOTAL NOI	$59,640.00	$0.00	$53,386.50	$0.00
NOTES	Mask occupies more than 1/2	Over built	Lease Expiration-2 years	3,592 SF outside yard

All information is to the best of ADCRE's knowledge and subject to change. Always consult your financial planner, CPA and other professionals when purchasing CRE.
Always consult your financial planner, CPA and other professionals when purchasing CRE.

Dan's Tour Selections

After numerous discussions to narrow Dan's options, Amanda sets a tour, which includes two office condo buildings, one simple freestanding building, and a plot of land in an ideal location. The land will only be toured if the buildings are a complete failure. Step three discusses narrowing the building prospects in preparation to make an offer.

STEP THREE

Property Tour, Seeing is Believing

Keywords: property tour, take notes, first impressions, parking, shared space, letter of intent, property owner's association, office flow, office culture, storage space, off-market, asset, portfolio, sale

Timeline: A tour date is usually set within one week of the property search. Plan on twenty to thirty minutes for each property.

Finally! Dan Campos, owner of Lifeline Insurance, is ready to tour. The company's parameters were defined, and multiple options were cut to the top four preferences.

DO THE MATH: Multiply each property times 30 minutes for total tour time.

4 buildings x 30 minutes (drive time is included in the 30 minutes) = 120 minutes or 2 hours.

Take Notes

Amanda hands Dan a notebook that outlines the day's adventure. Dan flips through the tabs and says, "I notice you have a page after each property for notes."

Amanda nods. "I find that by the end of the day, the properties blend together. I'll take notes regarding the broker's comments as well as yours. You may want to make a few for reference later. I always refer back to our notes when we start negotiations and draft the *letter of intent.*"

Industry Lingo: A *letter of intent* is a non-binding meeting of the minds between buyer and seller regarding basic sale terms such as price, earnest monies, due diligence period, title company, closing period, etc.

First Impressions

Amanda starts the tour at a large office condo project. She shares how important it is to observe everything from the parking lot to building signage to the exterior and interior appearance. She points to the building exterior. "Note the condition of the building and the grounds; they appear well maintained. That indicates the POA, property owner's association, is doing their job."

Industry Lingo: *POA*, property owner's association, is like a residential HOA or homeowner's association. Often in commercial real estate it is referred to as HOA as well.

SIMPLY OWN IT!

Amanda suggests Dan snap a photo of the office complex directory and note synergistic businesses, along with surrounding amenities. Dan does not require signage for his company, yet Amanda pipes in.

"I like this property because it offers prominent signage on a main street and, for resale, this is a big advantage. Also, there's drive-up parking and easy access. Both add value to the property in the future when you implement an exit strategy."

Dan and Amanda enter the building. It has high exposed ceilings and an open floor plan. It reminds Dan of creative warehouse conversions. "I know this look is trending right now, yet it doesn't work for our company culture. It's too open and noisy. We need private offices."

Amanda gestures toward a wall with an expansive window line, "This portion of the building would be great for a row of offices, and the common area workspace would still have a lot of light with side windows in the offices. If you like the area, a space planner can easily draw up a sketch."

Dan shakes his head. "Thanks, not my style, and I suspect it'll cost a pretty penny to convert."

"Next!" Amanda says, and they drive to the next property, a freestanding, well-appointed office. Dan is open minded, but it is not his first choice because the renovations will be significant.

Make sure to include these observations and answers to questions in your notes:

- What are the pros and cons of the building, both exterior and interior?
- How many covered and open parking spaces are there?
- Is signage allowed on the building?
- Is there a monument sign you can use?
- What amenities are in the area?

- Is there any common area space or on-site storage?
- Note condition of major improvements, parking lot, roof, building deterioration
- What is the IT capacity?
- Who is the electric provider, and how much power is allocated to your building or unit?
- If there is a floor plan showing where the offices are, take a minute to sketch how to make it your own.
- Is the window line sufficient for your needs?

Parking

Note if the parking lot is full in the middle of the day. This may indicate limited parking for employees and clients. Diplomatically address concerns with the seller's rep. Is there ample parking for visitors close to the building entrance? What is the ratio of covered reserved parking to unreserved parking, and is there underground parking? How many covered reserved parking spaces come with the property if it is a condominium? For a fee simple property, if you are considering solar panels, solar companies may install panels as covered parking.

Don't Judge a Book by Its Cover

When touring a shabby building, don't focus on the dated carpet or scratched paint. Instead, focus on the layout, the number of windows, and the flow of the space. If the building has an odor, it may be from pets at the office or sewage concerns. New carpet, paint, and minor buyer improvements are minimal expenditures compared to adding in a row of six offices and a drop ceiling, as the first property Dan toured would have required. Often a lender will incorporate renovation prices into the property loan, saving a buyer this additional upfront cost.

The Property

Amanda locks up the office, and they proceed to the next location. Property three stands out to Dan, even though it was built in the 1980s and needs some TLC.

This two-story, 15,000-square-foot Tuscan style office is adorned with lush, albeit overgrown, landscaping. It is close to a major freeway access point yet has minimal visibility from the road. One reason Dan is drawn to it is because it is tucked away and has a resort feel from the past. Some roof tiles are cracked, and the outside begs for a coat of paint.

"I like it," Dan says.

Amanda comments, "I've been dying to see this building ever since I started selling commercial real estate, but it's only had one owner. Let's see if the inside is as captivating."

She presses the keypad, and the door opens. Amanda flips on the lights. Unlike the outside, the inside is meticulous and well kept. A grand staircase leads to the second floor; an elevator is hidden from view.

"I can't believe the owner didn't throw some paint on the outside for curb appeal," Dan says, shrugging his shoulders and shaking his head.

"Between the dilapidated exterior and the poor quality of photos, it's no wonder this property is sitting on the market for five months in a hot market," Amanda comments with a sparkle. "I see it as an opportunity for us."

Behind the reception area and the staircase, the suite opens to offices and an extensive window line. Dan can imagine his company in this space. Mentally, he assigns an office to each employee. The upstairs can be used for his sales staff. The breakroom needs a facelift yet is centrally located and near the conference room, perfect for meetings. The space is growing on Dan.

Amanda mentions to him, "I've observed that more waking hours are spent at the office than at home and yet, usually, more thought is allocated to designing our home than our office. You can design the property so you enjoy it as much as your home. It also has room for growth or a possible tenant."

Amanda and Dan step into the comfortable classic oak conference room and discuss the office flow, Dan's business culture, and the timing of a potential purchase and move-in date. The future office of Lifeline Insurance begins to take form.

Office Flow

Does the space need to be reconfigured to maximize the business operation? Do you need more collaborative open space or more offices? Space planners design buyers' renovation ideas into concrete blueprints. Dream big and pull back if you exceed your budget. Contractors will provide a free guesstimate of your remodel. For a minimal cost, a space plan helps them see your vision and provides a more accurate preliminary bid.

Office Culture

Do your employees expect a separate, collaborative workspace? Does the company culture require individual offices or open areas? Current office trends designate space for employees' creative inspiration, or downtime, such as a lounge. This collaborative space may be incorporated in the breakroom, the conference area, or the reception area.

Storage Space

Storage space is often overlooked when touring a property. No matter what company I have worked for, the office lacked onsite storage. Look for "dead" space that can be used for storage, such as at the end of a long hallway.

Perhaps storage can be added to an oversized office. When you meet with the space planner, ask them how to efficiently design a storage closet.

Other Considerations

Are the window coverings adequate for your use? Are there blinds to shade the intense sun during peak exposure? What condition are the blinds in? In Dan's case, when he trims the overgrown landscaping, will window coverings be needed to limit the early morning or late afternoon sun?

Take a minute to look up. Stained ceiling tiles often indicate a roof leak or HVAC condensation. Regardless of the cause, make note of it, and then have the building inspector investigate the source of the leak and estimate the cost of repair during your due diligence period.

Is the suite wired for IT and phones? Note the server/phone room location. Is it adequately ventilated with air conditioning, allowing it to be secured?

Off-Market Space

During your tour, the seller's rep may mention an *off-market* building for sale. A commercial space isn't actively marketed until a seller signs an employment contract with a listing broker and it is entered into the brokerage database. This off-market space may be the best fit for the buyer.

Industry Lingo: *Off-market* is an unlisted property. AKA: pocket listing.

CPA Involvement

Buying a commercial building affords multiple tax benefits. A CPA can assist with how the building purchase benefits your overall business goals. They will verify the lease versus purchase model as well as calculate and suggest tax write-offs. If you are remodeling, one suggestion may be cost segregation, which reduces taxes by depreciating building improvements over three to five years versus thirty-nine years. The CPA will assess if your company benefits by leasing the building back to the business. She may also suggest that you take title of the property in a separate LLC to reduce unforeseen potential future liabilities. When you are selling a property prior to buying your new building, ask if a 1031 tax deferred exchange is the best choice for you.

Financial Advisor Questions

Talk with your financial advisor about how building ownership fits into your long-term business plan and retirement strategy. Discuss if your newly formed LLC should be in your name or within your family trust. Does placing your LLC within the family trust protect your heirs from probate? Often these strategy meetings overlap with your CPA planning.

Buyer Credibility

No seller wants to go under contract with a looky-loo buyer. Presenting the seller with a strong buyer is necessary to secure the deal and move toward a successful close, especially in a tight market with slim inventory. A qualified buyer rep appropriately markets their buyer's value to a seller on initial contact with the listing broker, the seller's representative. Until the property has a fully executed purchase contract and escrow has been opened, the property can be sold to another buyer. It behooves a buyer to prepare upfront to verify their buying strength.

Amanda establishes Dan's credibility in an email sent to a listing broker.

> *Hi Steve—we have a buyer proactively speaking with his lender who needs at least a 10,000 SF building in Gilbert. Please forward all possible options. We're touring early next week.*

This simple email sets the stage for any seller's broker. Frank, the seller's rep, is optimistic about the prospective buyer even before Lifeline Insurance tours because they prequalified with a lender. When Amanda speaks with Frank to confirm the tour, she reiterates that her buyer, Dan, is prequalified and will put down 20 percent of the acquisition price. Yes, Lifeline Insurance is a desirable buyer, and this will work in their favor during negotiations in a tight market.

Business Owner Tip: A lender's prequalification letter isn't always that easy for a buyer to secure until a property is identified, and the purchase specifics are outlined. To start the lending process, a buyer has a better chance of getting a prequalification letter from their regular bank. The lender may provide a prequalification letter with a loan price range based on initial financial information the buyer delivers prior to underwriting the loan.

$$$ Saving Tip: Once the property is under contract, the buyer can shop around for the best lender deal. Do NOT release your earnest monies until you are fully qualified for your loan.

Prequalifying Buyers

A buyer doesn't have to have financing pinned down prior to finding a building to be positioned favorably in the seller's eyes.

Hi Julie—A well-known local law firm, in business for over fifteen years, would like to purchase a 5,000 SF high-end office. Can you please forward me any properties that might work for my client?

Amanda speaks with Julie and reiterates the buyer is a prestigious, upstanding law firm within the community and is ranked Scottsdale's number one family law practice. The client's strength is reaffirmed, and Julie is excited about the prospective buyer because she knows of the law firm. Amanda adds that she has introduced the buyer to a strong local lender.

Conversely, if the buyer does not have any buying history, there are still effective ways to market a potential buyer.

Hi Rockwell—An auto repair shop, in business for ten years, that works on high end automobiles, requires 15,000 SF of warehouse space in Deer Valley. They need three or more roll up doors as well as a small, fenced yard. He is proactively talking with a lender about Small Business Administration (SBA) financing from Mid-First Bank. Thanks for emailing possible options ASAP.

An experienced buyer rep attractively sells the buyer's assets, or value, upfront. In this email example, the ten-year auto repair shop doesn't own a commercial building yet. By stating he has a long term rental history and a loyal following, the seller knows the business owner has a reasonable chance at securing financing through a government financed SBA lending program.

When inventory for commercial property is low, and it's a seller's market, sellers get very particular about which buyer they choose to enter into a purchase contract. Sellers prefer a buyer with past buying history, cash, and/or a lender's prequalification.

Submitting an Offer and Lending

The property tour comes to a close and nets a win for Dan. Gilbert Professional is a surprise addition to the original tour. An alert using Dan's parameters on Amanda's commercial database informs her of a new listing in Dan's complex. Experienced brokers will set alerts for client parameters for daily market updates.

Dan wants to keep his company in the Gilbert Professional office condos, where his current office is located. This larger building within the complex checks off everything on his wish list. Dan asks Amanda to write a letter of intent (*LOI*) immediately to purchase the 10,500-square-foot office condo, and she goes right to work. It is tricky presenting an offer on a new listing. Amanda knows that sellers commonly think their property is undervalued when an offer is generated quickly. Additionally, she doesn't want to tip the buyer's hand that the property—with minor modifications—is a perfect fit for Dan.

Industry Lingo: *LOI* is an acronym for a *letter of intent*. The LOI is the starting point to negotiate basic sale terms.

Seller's Intentions

Back at the office, before Amanda drafts the LOI for Dan to review, she asks the listing broker why the building is being sold. Additionally, she tests the broker to see what terms the seller anticipates with an offer. In step four, the information Amanda gathers will influence the LOI she drafts on Dan's behalf.

STEP FOUR

Patience, the Letter of Intent

Keywords: letter of intent, LOI, request for proposal, RFP, project or building, buyer, saleable square footage, buyer improvements, mortgage payment, parking, identity or signage, agency disclosure and brokerage, strategy

Timeframe: Negotiating a letter of intent may take up to two weeks. Be patient.

Amanda and Dan have discussed Lifeline Insurance's search parameters, identified possible purchase options, organized tours of selected properties, chosen a building, and are now preparing for the next step: negotiating the sales terms and presenting the initial offer to buy the building, known as a letter of intent (LOI).

The LOI is an opportunity to outline the buyer's strengths, summarize purchase terms, and set the tone of negotiations. Negotiations may go back and forth several times. For many, this is nerve racking, especially if the seller has another offer on the table. An experienced buyer rep will advise a buyer when the seller has reached their limit in the negotiations. The buyer will need to assess if the deal is acceptable and affordable.

LOI's can be generated by the buyer or the seller. When a buyer asks the seller for a proposal, it is called a request for proposal or an RFP. Neither the LOI or the RFP are intended to be a commitment by either party; rather, they lay a foundation for further discussions and drafting the purchase and sale agreement (PSA).

It's All Negotiable

Every section in an LOI is negotiable. The entire PSA is negotiable. Everything is negotiable until both parties fully execute the PSA. Contract terms can be renegotiated after escrow is opened provided both parties agree, and it is in writing.

LOI's Include the Following Key Negotiation Points:

- *Purchase Price (cash or finance):* The sale price may be more favorable for the buyer if they pay cash versus finance.
- *Earnest Deposit:* Sellers want buyers to have something at stake while the property is under contract, and this is money. The more money a buyer is comfortable putting in escrow through their refundable due diligence period, the more a seller takes them seriously.
- *Escrow Company and Title Officer:* Identify what third party escrow company will handle the sale transaction and transfer of title. This process differs depending on if the transaction occurs in a title state or an attorney

state. See Step Five for basic differences between the two ways of transferring real estate.

- *Due Diligence Period (Inspection Period):* This identifies how long the buyer has to do their homework while their earnest monies are *fully* refundable. To get a seller's attention, tighten the due diligence period as short as possible. Obtaining financing is often included in the due diligence period, yet it can be broken out separately depending on the temperaments of seller and buyer.
- *Required Due Diligence Items:* These are the items that a buyer requests from the seller to analyze the property and make an educated purchase decision.
- *Close of Escrow:* This time period starts after the due diligence period expires and earnest monies become non-refundable. It is used to prepare loan and title documents for the transfer of title at closing. If the buyer wants an aggressive price or is in a sellers' market, one way to secure the purchase is to reduce the time to close.
- *Closing Costs:* This section outlines who pays closing costs, sales transfer fees, property owners' association fees, etc. If your buyer really wants the property, suggest they pay more than customary for closing costs.
- *Purchase and Sale Agreement (PSA):* This defines if the buyer or seller initially prepares the PSA for the other party to review. This is traditionally prepared by the

seller, yet a buyer can proactively present a PSA to the seller for review.

- *Agency Disclosure and Brokerage*—This identifies which brokerage firm represents whom, how commission is split, and when the brokers are paid. It is customary for the seller to pay both brokers' commissions at the close of escrow. However, a buyer can pay their rep's commission independently to sweeten the deal for the seller.

Additional LOI Considerations for Negotiations:

- *Other Conditions:* Typically, the buyer is responsible for any property inspections. One exception is when the buyer requests the seller pay for a current ALTA survey and/or a Phase I report instead of having the purchaser pay these customary buyer costs.
- *1031 Exchange:* If the buyer has sold a property within the past 45 days and is entering into a 1031 tax deferred exchange, note that the seller will cooperate with the buyer's 1031 during the sale process.
- *Contingency:* An example would be a buyer who purchases the property before their existing lease expires and asks the seller to leaseback the building for six months after closing.

LOI Strategy

The LOI is comprised of many elements from initial introductions through ongoing interactions. If Dan of Lifeline Insurance is interested in more than one property, Amanda will write an offer on both properties. In Dan's case, there is only one option. Amanda gathers information on the listing broker and the seller, such as their personality, business style, and objectives, to develop a negotiation strategy. This accumulated knowledge is used to strategically draft the LOI.

The LOI is not written in stone. As stated earlier, each item in the LOI is a potential negotiation tool. In step one, Dan outlined key items for his new office. Now it is time to structure the LOI to emphasize Lifeline's financial strength to the seller.

Negotiation Considerations:

1. Is it a buyers or sellers market?
2. Who is the owner, and why are they selling?
3. How long has the property been on the market?
4. What is the condition of the building?
5. How old is the building?
6. What are property comparables from like buildings in the area over the last six to twelve months?
7. What does your broker know about the listing broker?

Please note that if Dan's property was on the market for over six months, Amanda would be more aggressive with the initial offer.

Dan's Draft LOI *(with Amanda's thought process in italics to discuss with Dan. This is not shared with the seller.)*

Buyer:	Lifeline Insurance
Property:	Gilbert Professional Offices, Unit 230 and 240 (+/- 10,500 SF)

Purchase Price: $2,992,000.00 *(Seller is asking $3,100,000.00 and the unit was just advertised for sale, so the seller has high expectations. A low-ball offer will kill the deal for Dan.)* Buyer is financing the purchase and will provide proof of funds once the LOI is agreed to. *(If proof of funds is presented with the LOI, and it shows the buyer has more money than the offer, a seller will assume that the buyer can pay more for the property.)*

Earnest Deposit: Upon execution of a Purchase and Sales Agreement (PSA) and opening of escrow, the Buyer will deposit $50,000.00 with the Escrow Agent. The earnest deposit shall be refundable, with no offset or deduction, if the Buyer elects for any reason to cancel the escrow prior to or upon expiration of the Buyer's Due Diligence Period. *(Different areas of the country have unwritten standards as to how much earnest money equals a sincere offer. In Dan's neck of the woods, $50,000 in earnest monies shows he is a legitimate, invested buyer.)*

Escrow Agent: Stewart Title and Trust (agent name and contact information). Escrow will be opened as soon as there is a fully executed PSA and the deposit of the $50,000.00 earnest monies. Earnest monies will remain in escrow until the close of escrow. *(Sometimes earnest monies are released to the seller after the due diligence period expires versus being held with the title company until closing. This is not recommend unless you have money to lose. When the purchase takes a wrong direction for the buyer after earnest monies go hard, demanding that the title company not release the funds to the seller may be the buyer's only recourse until the dispute is settled. Anticipate that if you make this demand, the seller may take legal action.)*

Due Diligence: Buyer shall have a period of thirty (30) days from receipt of due diligence items and opening escrow to determine if the Property is suitable for Buyer's purposes. *(Amanda wants to keep the timeframe as tight as possible, while still giving Dan time to properly inspect the office condo and have his financing approved. The due diligence period can be any agreed upon timeframe.)*

The following items that the Seller has in their possession will be provided to the Buyer at the Seller's expense within five (5) business days or sooner:

- Building plans, architectural drawings, and/or CAD's.
- CC&R's, Amendments, Bylaws, and parking allocations.
- Real Estate Tax Bills or estimated taxes and any notices of proposed valuations.
- Survey and/or recorded plat map.
- Phase 1 or environmental seller questionnaire
- Any shared access agreement and parking easements.
- HOA fees, budget, and capital expenditure study.
- Last year of electric bills
- Mail box location
- Any other documents that are part of the property.

Throughout the Due Diligence Period, the Seller shall comply with any reasonable requests from the Buyer for additional due diligence information that might be in the physical possession of the Seller, and provided that any such information/documentation is pertinent and specific to the property.

In the event Buyer elects to move forward, the earnest money and any interest earned thereon shall be considered non-refundable, except in the event of a default by the Seller or as otherwise provided in the PSA, and will be credited toward the sales price upon close of escrow.

In the event Buyer elects to cancel escrow during the Due Diligence Period, a written notice must be sent to the Escrow Agent and all earnest money with any interest earned thereon will be returned to the Buyer, the PSA will be terminated, and the Buyer and Seller shall have no further obligation to each other.

Close of Escrow: The closing date will be two (2) weeks after the completion of the due diligence period. *(Amanda spoke with Dan's lender and the title company to affirm the lender can meet the timeframes laid out in the LOI. The strategy is to show the seller Dan is committed to a quick six-week close once escrow is opened. Amanda knows most financed offers will take up to three (3) months to close.)*

Warranties and Representations: The Seller will allow the Buyer to make all reasonable efforts to investigate to its own satisfaction the physical condition(s) and or integrity of the building, as well as the financial position of the property. All warranties that are still active will be transferred to the Buyer at the time of close.

Other Conditions:	The Buyer is responsible for any costs related to any property inspections.
Agency Representation:	The Buyer and Seller recognize that Amanda Davis, with Davis Commercial, exclusively represents the Buyer. Davis Commercial will be paid a 3 percent commission per a separate agreement at the close of escrow out of seller's proceeds. *(A commission for the buyer's representative is seldom negotiable when selling a building. The listing agent signed an employment contract with the seller prior to putting the building on the market that dictates what both brokers are paid. This is generally a fifty/fifty split.)*
Confidentiality:	The parties hereto will maintain the confidentiality of the items of the transaction and the contents of this letter and transaction documentation.
Sales Agreement:	Based upon a general understanding of terms of sale by both parties, the Seller, at its expense, shall deliver to the Buyer within three (3) business days, or sooner, from the execution hereof a PSA for its review and execution. If seller prefers, Buyer's rep will draft the PSA from the Arizona Association of Realtors forms. *(Since either party can prepare PSA, Amanda offers to draft it to show the seller the buyer is a committed buyer and ready to open escrow ASAP, thus shielding off another offer. Please note, not every state allows a real estate agent to draft contracts.)*
Expiration of Offer:	If the Seller and/or its agent have not responded to this letter of interest, verbally and/or in writing, by Tuesday, August thirteenth at four p.m., Buyer's interest may expire.

Dan's offer should get the seller's attention—at least enough to encourage the seller to counter and move the negotiations a step closer to drafting a PSA. Here are three good reasons the seller will counter:

1. The purchase price is close to the asking price.
2. The buyer will show proof of funds.
3. The closing timeline is brief compared to most commercial closings.

Why bother with an LOI instead of going right to a purchase contract? Purchase and sale contracts are often lengthy and costly. It behooves seller and buyer to be on the same page with key purchase points before attorneys get involved. By agreeing to the main points in the brief letter of intent, both parties reduce the amount of time it requires attorneys to negotiate the fine points of the lengthy PSA.

Luck of the Draw

Amanda calls the seller's broker before submitting the LOI to gather any last-minute insights. As luck will have it, another offer is anticipated by the end of the day. This is a buyer's worst nightmare, to be caught in a bidding war with another eager buyer. After a discussion with Dan, Amanda amends the LOI in key areas to read:

Purchase Price:	$3,050,000 *versus* $2,992,000 *(Seller is asking $3,100,000.00.)*
Earnest Deposit:	Upon execution of a Purchase and Sales Agreement (PSA) and opening of escrow, the Buyer will deposit $100,000 *versus* $50,000 with the Escrow Agent. Attached is the buyer's proof of funds for $3,050,000.
Close of Escrow:	The closing date will be two (2) weeks after the completion of the due diligence period or (***Amanda adds***) as soon as possible.

Both Amanda and Dan believe that this offer will generate a counter and hopefully an acceptance of terms. Amanda runs the comparables again and believes that even if Dan pays the full asking price, the property will appraise for financing. Dan is prepared to pay the full asking price.

Due to the complexity of many commercial transactions, often the seller is given a few days to respond. In this case, time is of the essence for Dan to get this property under contract. Amanda gives the seller one day to respond. Once this final adjustment is made, Amanda emails the offer to the listing broker, she provides proof of funds with the LOI and follows up with a call to verbally highlight Dan's attractive terms. She also emphasizes that an answer is needed in twenty-four hours. The listing broker calls Amanda the following day and states that the seller will accept Dan's offer. They will draft a PSA to review by the end of the week.

This takes us to step five—the PSA and the title company.

STEP FIVE
The PSA and The Title/Escrow Company

Keywords: Purchase and Sales Agreement (PSA), purchase contract, title state, attorney state, title company, escrow agent, Schedule B, Standard ALTA Owners Policy, Extended Owner's Policy, ALTA survey

Timeline: thirty to ninety days or more depending on purchase contract and what is discovered during the inspection period

The Purchase and Sales Agreement (PSA)

The buyer, Lifeline Insurance, and seller have accepted and signed off on the LOI terms. These terms are sent to the seller's attorney to draft a PSA for review. Dan hires a commercial real estate attorney to review the PSA to assure his interests are protected. Amanda also reviews the PSA and compares it to the agreed-upon LOI. Any discrepancies or comments are sent to Dan's attorney for consideration. PSA negotiations take a few rounds for attorneys to hammer out the legalese on behalf of their client. Once the purchase contract details are agreed upon by both parties, signatures are gathered and a fully executed contract is sent to title with the request to open a new escrow file.

Now it's time to dig into the due diligence period and confirm that the property meets their business and personal requirements. While this stage is routinely acknowledged as an important step in any real estate purchase, what the process entails can sometimes be unclear. During the due diligence period the key players will be the lender, title company, inspectors, brokers, and seller to determine if the desired use of the property is feasible. Step five discusses the title company's vital role in the transaction as a third party. Step six is about the lender's role and the buyer's due diligence.

What Role Does a Title Company Play?

A title company plays several key roles in a real estate transaction. It acts as an impartial third party between the buyer, the seller, the title insurance company, and the mortgage lender. The title company is responsible for researching previous and current title holders of the property, providing title insurance, and working with the lender through closing, assuring the buyer and seller a clean transfer of title.

Before the title company issues the insurance policy, if they are using an agent, they contract with the title company to underwrite the policy. Some title companies are title agents while others are actual title companies such as Stewart Title & Trust or First American Title. In addition, there are escrow only companies. If you choose to use an escrow only company, they request title from the title company and the two companies work together. Most of this is done behind the sense for the buyer.

A 2-week close

An eager buyer and seller set an ambitious closing timeline of fifteen days from opening escrow. The buyer won the bid with a promise to close quickly. They signed the PSA and opened escrow. Earnest monies were deposited, and the fifteen-day clock started ticking.

A week later the title company informed both parties that the title commitment report and Schedule B, discussed in detail further down, would not be ready for another week due to a high volume of transactions. This delay made title review impossible for the buyer's attorney prior to the scheduled closing date. There was no time to object to potential issues on the title report, such as outdated recorded leases, property liens, antiquated zoning overlays, etc. To sell the property, both buyer and seller agreed to extend the closing date.

Title Company versus Escrow Company

To add to some of the title mystery, the words "title" and "escrow" are often misused. While many people think the terms are interchangeable, they are two very different parts of the real estate transaction.

Title is an owner's legal right to own, use, and dispose of a property. Having clean title is crucial to any real estate transaction. During this process, a title company works to authenticate that the seller has proper ownership of the property and help the buyer obtain title insurance to protect them from financial loss and legal expenses in the event there is a defect in the title.

Escrow, on the other hand, is the arrangement of a neutral third party holding and managing the payment of funds required for two parties in a transaction. The escrow company is responsible for making sure the money goes to all the correct places when terms of the contract are met. The buyer and seller work with an escrow agent, who serves as the principal person involved in the transaction. Escrow agents, or officers, have a solid understanding of the entire transaction and possess the skills necessary for a smooth closing. They are responsible for closing the transaction once all purchase contract conditions are met.

Escrow State and Attorney State

There are two ways to close on a commercial property in the U.S.: in an escrow state or an attorney state. The determination as to how your property will go through the escrow process ultimately depends on where the property is located. In an escrow state, a big part of the closing process in an escrow state is handled at the escrow company versus by attorneys.

Most of the states in the Northeast and Southeast have laws that mandate the presence of an attorney to facilitate a real estate closing. In these "attorney states," closing attorneys represent each side of the sale and replace the escrow company. These attorneys generally will not negotiate the contract between buyer or seller. Instead, they act as a neutral third party to validate both the buyer and seller's conditions are met before transferring the property's title to the buyer. The closing attorney can work for your lender, title insurance company, or on their own.

Attorney states include Alabama, Connecticut, Delaware, District of Columbia, Florida, Georgia, Kansas, Kentucky, Maine, Maryland, Massachusetts, Mississippi, New Hampshire, New Jersey, New York, North Dakota, Pennsylvania, Rhode Island, South Carolina, Vermont, Virginia, and West Virginia.

All other states are escrow states. Instead of a closing attorney, escrow states use escrow officers or title agents to handle the closing of the property. Below is a color-coded map showing escrow and attorney states.

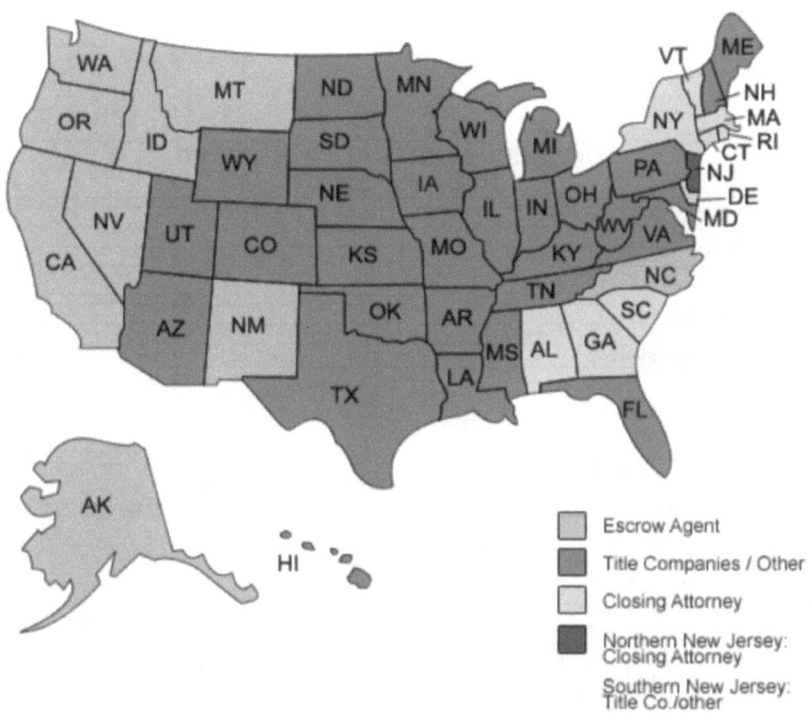

Source: American Bar Association

Title companies in escrow states and attorney states differ in the services they offer throughout the transaction process. In an attorney state, an attorney reviews and interprets critical dates in the PSA. In an escrow state like Arizona, the title company's escrow agent translates the important contract dates into a brief critical date letter for all parties to review and agree upon. This is a helpful tool for buyer and seller to meet important deadlines. If your title company does not provide this service, ask your buyer rep to prepare one. Below is one example of a critical date letter. If you are in an attorney state, one of the attorneys may provide one.

stewart title

Real partners. Real possibilities.

Stewart Title & Trust of Phoenix, Inc.
2930 E Camelback, Ste 210
Phoenix, AZ 85016
(602) 462-8068 direct   (928) 496-2089 fax
Jennifer.Langford@stewart.com

Escrow Officer: Jennifer Langford
Phone: (602) 462-8068
Email: Jennifer.Langford@stewart.com

COMMERCIAL CRITICAL DATE LETTER
FILE NO.: 1289804

Address:	8160 E Butherus Drive Unit 5		Agreement Date:	6/11/2021	
Parcel:	215-55-062				
Selling Agent:	N/A		Listing Agent:	Andrea Davis CRE	
Property Type:	Commercial				
Seller:	Stuart J. Spivak				
Buyer:	Healing Wounds, LLC, and/or assignee				

Transaction Event	Time Frame	Due Date	Section	Completed
Contract Acceptance Date:	Date contract accepted and executed by Seller and delivered to Broker in Section 9p	6/10/2021 *Contract Signed By Seller 6/11/2021	Lines 41 thru 43	6/11/2021
Earnest Money Deposit $20,000.00	No later than 5 days after Contract Acceptance	6/16/2021	Lines 35 thru 37	6/16/2021
Commercial Seller's Property Disclosure Statement Seller to deliver completed SPDS to Buyer. *Buyer shall provide Seller notice of any disapproved SPDS items within the Due Diligence Period or 5 days after receipt of SPDS, whichever is later.*	Within 5 days after Contract Acceptance	6/16/2021	Lines 74 thru 76	6/16/2021
Additional Seller Disclosures and Information Seller to provide to Buyer disclosures and information pertinent to property in writing as described on lines 79 -90. *Buyer shall provide Seller with written notice of any disapproved Seller disclosure or information items prior to expiration of Due Diligence Period or 5 days after receipt, whichever is later.* NO ESTOPPELS will be delivered.	Within 10 days after Contract Acceptance	6/21/2021	Lines 77 thru 95	
Affidavit of Disclosure If applicable, Seller shall deliver completed Affidavit of Disclosure to Buyer. *Buyer shall provide Seller notice of any disapproved Affidavit of Disclosure items within the Due Diligence Period or 5 days after receipt of the Affidavit of Disclosure, whichever is later.*	Within 5 days after Contract Acceptance	6/16/2021	Lines 96 thru 99	6/16/2021
Due Diligence Period Buyer shall deliver to Seller signed notice of any items that are disapproved and state in the notice the election of Buyer as provided in Lines 130-150 Buyer failure to give notice of disapproved items or cancellation of this contract within the specified time period shall be deemed as Buyer's election to proceed as provided in Lines 153-155.	30 days after Contract Acceptance	7/11/2021	Lines 126 thru 129	
Inspections	During Due Diligence Period	7/11/2021	Lines 160 thru 184	
Title Commitment Due	Within 15 days after Contract Acceptance	6/28/2021	Lines 245 thru 249	6/22/2021
Title Review Period Buyer shall provide notice of any items disapproved to Seller as provided for in Lines 250 -253	Until expiration of the Due Diligence Period	7/11/2021	Lines 250 thru 253	
Financing Commitment Contingency Period	30 days after Contract acceptance	7/11/2021	Lines 231-237	
Close of Escrow * August 25th is a Wednesday	If Closing Date is a Holiday-extend to next Business Day	8/25/2021 Or anytime between 8/25/2021 and	Lines 56 thru 59 Lines 380 thru 392	

Schedule B, Part of the Title Commitment

Before closing, the buyer will receive a copy of the title commitments and have several days to review it. Depending on where the property is located, the title commitments could vary slightly but will always include the current status of the title in the Schedule A, Schedule B, Requirements and Exceptions.

An important part of the title commitment is Schedule B, which contains the requirements, exceptions, and exclusions to the title policy. Buyers should pay close attention to this section, as it lists everything that must be completed or adhered to for title insurance to be issued. If one of the requirements cannot be met for whatever reason, it will affect escrow. Examples of requirements include:

- Tax payments.
- Proof of identity.
- Release of liens.
- Recording the new deed.
- Recording the loan documents.

Even if the state you're purchasing the property in doesn't require legal representation to complete the transaction, it's advisable to seek legal counsel. Neither a real estate agent nor title insurance companies can provide legal advice about a property sale.

No matter how small, any title issues need to be resolved at the seller's expense in order to deliver a clear title to the buyer. This includes liens, old leases, past encroachments, and other unnecessary items.

Herman found a quaint 4,500-square-foot fee simple office building on three acres that he wanted to purchase for his doggie daycare business. The property had been in one family since it was built in the 1950s. When the attorney reviewed the Schedule B, he noticed a road easement through the middle of the property and the east side of the building. Fortunately for Herman, further digging revealed the easement had been abandoned by the municipality five years earlier. Recording the abandonment was required to clear the title. This formality added another four weeks to the close date.

Standard ALTA (American Land Title Association) Owner's Policy versus Extended/Enhanced Owner's Policy

Unlike other types of insurance such as auto or health that protect against circumstances that could happen in the future, title insurance protects against situations that happened in the past, such as unpaid taxes or liens against the property. There are two types of title insurance coverage: Standard ALTA Owner's Policy and Extended/Enhanced Owner's Policy.

A standard policy insures primarily against defects and liens in the history of the title through the date and time your deed is recorded. Although each state has individual policy limitations, this standard coverage policy is the most widely used type of title insurance. A defect may be an incorrect address, bankruptcy, forgery, boundary dispute, illegal deed, etc.

An extended owner's policy, sometimes called an enhanced owner's policy, insures against matters that cannot be determined by an examination of public record. Examples include zoning and property restriction problems, a previous owner remodeling without required building permits, unrecorded mechanic liens, and a host of other issues. A current ALTA survey is required for an extended owner's policy, so plan appropriately for this during your due diligence period.

$$$ Saving Tip: Check with the local municipality early on to verify what type of zoning is required for your business.

For instance, a retail use cannot go into an office building unless it is zoned for mixed-use.

Below are a few examples for when it may be prudent to buy extended coverage:

- Lien claims on the property that may be complicated by bankruptcy issues.
- Concerns that title-related problems may occur after the policy's effective date. Standard title insurance only covers events or acts before the policy effectiveness date.
- Possibility of easements and encumbrances that are not recorded.
- Potential zoning violations.
- An older property with a long history of different uses and owners.

Business Tip: Avoid confusing an ALTA Owner's Policy with an ALTA survey. The owner's policy is title insurance, and the ALTA survey is a detailed land survey map.

Stewart Title and Trust was kind enough to share the chart below, showing the difference in insurance coverage under a standard policy versus an extended owner's policy.

COMPARING COVERAGE
OF ALTA'S STANDARD AND EXTENDED OWNER'S AND HOMEOWNER'S POLICIES

In Arizona, Stewart Title & Trust offers customers several levels of coverage for policyholders' protection. The standard policy covers you for defects and liens in the history of your title not excepted to in the policy through the date and time your deed is recorded in the public records. The extended owner's policy is designed to provide protection against loss resulting from survey matters and mechanics liens. The ALTA® homeowner's policy provides enhanced coverage, which protects you from additional risks, including some that might occur after the deed is recorded. The homeowner's policy is available only on 1-4 family properties located on a platted subdivision lot.

Head-to-head Coverage Comparison

Coverages Included Without Endorsement Assumes compliance with Stewart Title's underwriting requirements for issuance of the applicable policy.	Standard Owner's Policy 2006	Extended Owner's Policy	Homeowner's Policy (12/2/13)
Covered Risks			
Third-party claims on the title	√	√	√
Prior forgery, fraud or duress affecting the title	√	√	√
Liens or encumbrances on the title (e.g., prior mortgage or deed of trust, state or federal tax lien, condominium or homeowners association lien)	√	√	√
Improperly executed documents	√	√	√
Defective recording of documents	√	√	√
Unmarketability of the title	√	√	√
Lack of a right of legal access to and from the land	√	√	√
Restrictive covenants limiting your use of the land	√	√	√
Gap coverage (extending coverage from the closing to the recording of the deed)	√	√	√
Duration			
Coverage continues as long as you own the property	√	√	√
Policy insures anyone who inherits the property from you	√	√	√
Policy insures the trustee of an estate-planning trust	√	√	√
Policy insures the beneficiaries of a trust upon your death	√	√	√
Extended Coverage			
Parties in possession of the property that are not disclosed by the public records (e.g., tenants, adverse possessors)	*	√	√
Unrecorded easements (e.g., prescriptive easements) affecting the property	*	√	√

*Not automatically included in the basic policy but may be available by extended coverage

Coverages Included Without Endorsement			
Encroachments that would be disclosed by a survey	*	√	√
Mechanics liens (a lien against the property due to nonpayment of work)	*	√	√
Taxes or special assessments that are not shown as liens in the public records	*		√

*Not automatically included in the basic policy but may be available by extended coverage

(continued on next page)

SIMPLY OWN IT!

Head-to-head Coverage Comparison *(continued)*

Coverages Included Without Endorsement Assumes compliance with Stewart Title's underwriting requirements for issuance of the applicable policy.	Standard Owner's Policy 2006	Extended Owner's Policy	Homeowner's Policy (12/2/13)
Additional Coverages			
Correction or removal of an existing violation of certain covenants, conditions or restrictions			√
Loss of your title resulting from a prior violation of a covenant, condition or restriction			√
Up to $10,000 if you are unable to obtain a building permit due to an existing violation of a subdivision law or regulation, or if you must correct an existing violation (subject to a deductible)			√
Up to $25,000 if you must remedy or remove an existing structure because it was built without a proper building permit (subject to a deductible)			√
Up to $25,000 if you must remedy or remove an existing structure due to an existing violation of a zoning law or zoning regulation (subject to a deductible)			√
Up to $5,000 if you must remove your existing structures due to their encroachment upon your neighbor's land (subject to a deductible)			√
Inability to use the land as a single-family residence because such use violates an existing zoning law or zoning regulation			√
Forced removal of your existing structures because they encroach upon an easement or over a setback line			√
Damage to existing structures due to the exercising of an existing right to use any easement affecting the land			√
Damage to improvements due to the exercising of an existing right to use the surface of the land for the extraction or development of minerals, water or any other substance			√
Attempted enforcement of discriminatory covenant			√
Supplemental taxes because of prior construction or change of ownership or use			√
Damages due to the residence's not being located at the address stated in the policy			√
Payment of substitute rent and relocation expenses if you cannot use your home because of a claim covered by the policy			√
Automatic increase in policy amount up to 150% of policy amount over five years			√
Post-Policy Coverages			
Forgery affecting the title	√	√	√
Unauthorized leases, contracts or options			√
Ownership claims			√
Easements or restrictions affecting your use of the land			√
Encroachment of neighbor's buildings onto your land			√

DANA MCDONALD
Business Development Officer
Cell: (480) 387-0106
Dana.McDonald@stewart.com
www.stewart.com/phoenix
2930 E. Camelback Road, Ste. 210
Phoenix, AZ 85016

stewart
title

If you are currently working with an agent, this is not meant as a solicitation.
This information is deemed reliable, but not guaranteed.

This information is provided for general informational purposes only, should not be solely relied upon, and is subject to change without notice.

Title Company Timing

A successful closing involves a team and takes time. Your title company will need between five and ten business days to acquire reports for the preliminary title commitment. Some municipalities may have a sophisticated online interactive system for pulling records, while in other cities it may be necessary to request the documents in person.

If buyer title objections are warranted, such as removal of an expired lease or an address change, the buyer must identify the objections in writing by the contract deadline and require the seller remedy them prior to closing. If the buyer fails to make objections by the deadline, they waive their right to object to adverse title issues. The title objection date often differs from the expiration of the due diligence period, so do not automatically lump them together.

Between gathering lender, seller, and buyer documents and correcting the buyer objections, this process can take anywhere from one to four weeks. A buyer rep will help the buyer plan for these critical dates.

Business Tip: When the due diligence dance does not come together as anticipated, the buyer can ask to extend the due diligence period and keep their earnest monies fully refundable. Or other terms can be arranged between buyer and seller. All changes to the original contract must be in writing, signed and forwarded to the title agency.

Extension Requests and Solutions to extend Due Diligence

Buyer Reasons to Request a Due Diligence Extension	Possible Solution for Seller Agreement
One of the many inspection reports are delayed. Have the inspector send an email explaining why the report is late.	Offer to release all other due diligence items except the one report that is outstanding.
The lender needs more time for underwriting. Ask your lender to write up the request for seller and explain why the additional time is needed.	Offer the seller additional earnest monies. Do NOT let earnest monies go nonrefundable until you have final approval from your lender
You did not receive due diligence items in a timely manner per PSA terms.	Have the seller extend the due diligence period in accordance with how late the due diligence items were delivered.
During the inspection period, a material defect was discovered, and more time is needed to assess solutions.	Present the problem to the seller and ask for an appropriate extension.

If the seller and buyer cannot come to terms on a due diligence extension, the buyer can play hard ball and tell the seller they will cancel escrow if an agreement is not reached. To do this, first have your buyer rep verbally send the message. If there is no response, send a written message to escrow advising you are canceling escrow and demand your earnest monies be returned in full. This will get the seller's attention. But before you go this route, make sure you are willing to live with the consequences. The seller may be okay with the cancelation.

Diane's Purchase Story

Diane had a vision to buy a property for her computer school and add a tenant to offset the mortgage payment. She found an ideal property, where the tenant's lease expiration coincided with the COE. They negotiated and signed a PSA, and opened escrow. During Diane's due diligence period, her tenant rep discovered the lease had a clause giving the tenant first right to purchase the building if a qualified buyer presented an offer.

Needless to say, this fact should have been disclosed upfront, yet neither the seller nor the seller's broker read the lease prior to listing the building for sale. They simply did not know the tenant possessed this right. The lease allowed the tenant two weeks to respond to the landlord's demand letter to buy the property or waive their right to purchase. This was a nerve-racking two weeks for Diane since the property aligned perfectly with her dream.

Diane's buyer rep immediately requested the due diligence period be extended by two weeks until this issue was resolved. Diane had no reason to initiate costly inspections before knowing the tenant's decision. Luckily for her, the tenant was close to retirement and had no desire to buy the building.

An experienced buyer rep guides the buyer through the delicate purchase maze that eventually leads to closing the sale or canceling it. The rep offers solutions as challenges and problems arise. Some problems won't be resolved to the buyer's expectations and, thus, a written cancelation notice must be sent to the title agency. And the process begins again. Not to be discouraged, that's what the team and due diligence period are for, to confirm the property is right for you.

Step Six explains the lenders' role and more about the due diligence process.

STEP SIX
The Lender and Due Diligence

Keywords: lender, mortgage broker, due diligence, financing, appraisal, ALTA survey, Phase I report, 1031 tax deferred exchange, cash, shop around

Timeline: *A buyer can start the lending process at any time during the transaction, yet earlier is prudent.*

Obtaining property has many facets, twists, and turns, each one demanding focus. The property inspections and title report review command quite a bit of a buyer's time, but, typically, obtaining financing consumes most of the buyer's due diligence period.

Lender and Title Teamwork

Due diligence can make or break the deal. While the process is lengthy, it is a critical step to uncover any hidden problems. If no problems are found or the issues are minor, then inspections can be finished before the due diligence deadline. However, if major problems are uncovered during inspection, it is in everyone's best interest to extend the timeframe and fix the problem(s). A problem might range from a low appraisal to deferred maintenance to unpaid taxes to unacceptable easements running through the parcel and so on.

Once problems are uncovered, a seller must disclose them to any new potential buyer, even if the current deal dies. Depending on the property, sellers may have a harder time finding a new buyer and for that reason will often work with the buyer to extend the deadline until after the repairs are made or compensated.

Buyer Financial Requirements

Commercial lenders have different lending programs, such as conventional loans and government-guaranteed loans, like a Small Business Administration loan. Loan options may differ in a variety of ways:

- Hands on assistance from the lender or mortgage broker.
- Interest rates.
- Upfront processing points and fees.
- Financial requirements to assess a borrower's credibility.
- The length of the mortgage term can fluctuate from five to thirty years.
- The loan may be amortized over ten to thirty years.
- The lender may or may not roll tenant improvement costs into the loan.

$$$ Saving Tip: It pays to shop around.

Joyce's Story

Joyce had a 4,000 SF office condo under contract and thought she had a good commercial loan at a 5 percent interest rate from her national bank. Other buyers were securing loans around 4 percent from local lenders. She reached out to a few mid-sized local lenders and secured a loan at 3.5 percent, with only one origination point versus two. Joyce's monthly payments for her million-dollar loan shifted from $5,850 a month to $5,000 a month. She directed the $10,000 annual savings toward other business expenses. To finalize the mortgage, Joyce agreed to move her business banking to the lender.

Of course, lending hasn't historically been this friendly, yet you get the drift. Shop around until you find the best deal for you.

1031 Tax Deferred Exchange

One benefit of obtaining a property is the 1031 tax deferred exchange. This vehicle allows a taxpayer to sell an investment or commercial real estate property and reinvest the proceeds in a similar, "like-kind" property that is equal to or greater in value. If the buyer has recently sold an investment property and plans on buying another, they can defer their capital gains.

$$$ Saving Tip: Once you have determined a 1031 tax deferred exchange is the right decision for the proceeds from your property sale, inform the title company and 1031 exchange company *prior* to closing on the property. Otherwise, you will not be entitled to the exchange, and your capital gains will be taxed.

As long as IRS rules are diligently followed, capital gains on the sale of the property will be postponed. A third party 1031 exchange facilitator is required and assures a buyer the IRS rules are followed. In addition to 1031 tax deferred exchange funds to buy a property, a business can use cash or financing. Lifeline Insurance will finance its new building with 15 percent down. They want to reserve cash for running the company, expansion, and a rainy day instead of having it tied up in real estate.

Cash Purchase

The quickest way to close on a property is cash. A benefit to paying cash is negotiating power and an expedited close process. The fastest I've seen a commercial property close was in two weeks during the holidays. The star team player who jumped through the most hoops was the escrow officer, yet all parties to the transaction had their work to do. Cash does not require an appraisal, survey, or environmental report, though all are advised.

What Hath COVID Wrought and the Value of Cash

COVID created the perfect storm in Scottsdale, Arizona, in 2020 and 2021, with more buyers than sellers. Within months, commercial buildings increased 20 percent in value and kept climbing due to migration of businesses, limited supply of buildings for sale, and lack of construction.

It was mid-December and a property under contract for the full asking price had just fallen out of escrow. Another buyer came in with an all-cash offer a bit below asking price and an expedited ten-day close. Because of third-party inspections, ten days to close is very ambitious on a commercial transaction. For tax purposes, it was attractive to the seller to close before the year ended, so he accepted the lower offer, even though he was advised he could get a higher price with a bit of patience.

The buyer knew the market and understood escalating values of commercial real estate property and the risk of waiving most of his inspections. His residential real estate business had expanded, and he was determined to purchase his next business location. The buyer opted for only a property inspection. A lender would have required an appraisal and environmental questionnaire. By paying cash versus financing the acquisition, the buyer shortened his closing timeline from eight weeks to two weeks.

While the property was in escrow, the buyer received two back up offers at full asking price. The buyer paying cash made all the difference in being the chosen one. After closing, the buyer opted to refinance the property with his lender and take advantage of historical low interest rates.

Business Owner Tip: Speak with your lender prior to submitting an LOI to find out firsthand how much time they need to get reports for the appraisal, ALTA survey, and Phase I report. Ask for more time than you need since this is a negotiating point in the LOI.

Initial Lender Contact Shop Around

Getting more than one bid for a commercial loan is as beneficial as when buying a car or hiring a contractor. Comparing one lender's terms against another provides assurances of an offer you can't refuse. If you are unsure, don't hesitate to ask your buyer rep for input on which option is better. It always pays to be patient and to use discretion during this key phase. When researching the right lender, keep in mind that commercial lenders may not finance all types of commercial properties. Some lenders only finance medical users, while others lean toward industrial properties. Additionally, some businesses do not qualify for financing such as the CBD and cannabis industry because marijuana remains illegal under federal law.

$$$ Saving Tip: Don't just shop around. Respectfully share with a lender that another lender is offering a special deal, such as a lower interest rate or no upfront points.

An experienced lender will ask questions to ensure they understand how the property you are interested in buying supports your business. Their questions may include:

- What are your goals for the property?
- What is your exit strategy?

You should ask questions of potential lenders too. The answers may vary greatly. Select a lender who best aligns with your business intentions. Ask:

- Do you understand my industry as a business?
- Is an SBA loan or a conventional loan better for my business, and why?
- What is the difference between an SBA 7A loan or an SBA 504 loan? Why, or why not?
- How much of the building do I need to occupy to be considered for an SBA loan?
- What is the interest rate?
- What is the amortization period?
- Are there any upfront points or loan initiation fees?
- What collateral do you require?
- How much down payment is required for an owner/user building?
- Can tenant improvements be financed with the property purchase?
- Are there prepayment penalties?
- What is the underwriting process, and what information do you need from me?
- How will my business be presented to the underwriter?

- What is the term sheet for the loan? (This summarizes the quantified loan amount, its repayment, and legal terms.)
- When will I know if my loan is approved?

Mortgage Broker versus Banker

When it comes to shopping for a loan, you may want to consider a mortgage broker. A loan officer from a bank can only present financing options their bank offers. Mortgage brokers have access to more than one lender's finance terms. They shop around for you and compare one loan option against another to help determine the best loan for you in relation to your business and personal goals.

A mortgage broker may charge a fee for their service beyond what the lending institution charges. Ask what their fee is to see if it justifies the value added when comparing loans.

A buyer's primary bank might very well be the best choice as a lender due to a previous banking relationship. Regardless, exploring more than one option confirms your banker will present advantageous lending terms.

Martha's Lending Wake-up Call

Martha had her new 8,000-square-foot office building under contract and had the ear of her business banker, Harry. He could finance her building under SBA with only 10 percent down at 6 percent interest over a fifteen-year period.

"To help out even more with the monthly 'nut,' we'll amortize the loan over twenty-five years and drop your monthly payment considerably," Harry said.

Martha was elated until she spoke with a commercial mortgage broker. The broker asked when she planned to retire and whether she had the liquidity to put down 20 percent of the purchase price.

"Yes, why do you ask?" Martha said.

"I'm sure I can find you a program that follows your retirement plan and saves you money." Intrigued, Martha asked for a proposal. The mortgage broker shared a financing package for less than 4.5 percent over ten years that would be amortized for twenty-five years. She would be required to put 20 percent down.

Martha had the $500,000 to put down, so she took advantage of the lower interest rate and reduced her monthly payment by another $4,000. The ten-year loan maturity worked for Martha because she planned to sell her business and building before then.

Behind the Scenes

If you have ever wondered what goes on behind the scenes after you've selected your lender, I'm here to pull the curtain back. First and foremost, your lender serves as an advocate for you as an intermediary to the underwriter. A good lender should have a solid understanding of what is happening in your industry and the knowledge to assess your credit risk.

Their job is to understand how you and your business measure up and mitigate any weaknesses in your next step of purchasing property. At the end of the day, it is important for lenders to engage with clients in open communication to build a trustworthy relationship to finalize the lending process.

What do Lenders Require?

As with most other types of loans you may have applied for, borrowers are asked to provide information to demonstrate their business and/ or personal financial strength. While some of the information requested is simple, such as providing contact information for your business, other pieces may require more planning and preparation from the applicant. The requirements for a commercial loan vary substantially from one financial institution to another. To ensure the process runs smoothly, be sure to ask each lender what they require for underwriting well in advance. Generally, lenders require two to three years of your personal and business financials and tax returns.

I Don't Qualify for a Loan

Traditional financing is not for everyone. Tough business years may not support a bank's rigid requirements. One option is for a trusted family member to buy the building and be the landlord until the business qualifies for a bank loan. Or the family member might want to be a partner in the commercial ownership opportunity.

A seller may consider a short-term carryback on the building. A *hard money loan* is another option. With either, interest rates are generally higher. A shorter payoff term is required due to a borrower's higher risk factor.

Industry Lingo: *Hard money* loans are backed by a "hard" asset, such as real estate. They're used for short-term financing. You'll need to turn to a private lender or individual investor, as these loans are not offered by traditional financial institutions. They can be quicker and easier to secure than traditional financing. The downside: they come with higher interest rates and fees, and a short repayment term.

Amrish needed a 12,000 SF flex building for his expanding parking app business. He found the perfect building with tenants in place to offset his mortgage and allow for future growth. Unfortunately, the combination of sudden business growth and an unscrupulous business partner maxed out his credit. His balance sheet did not support conventional lending.

A savvy hard-money lender admired Amrish's character and drive and knew that his company was the way of the future. Amrish secured a five-year hard money loan at 6.5 percent instead of 3.5 percent conventional funding. The numbers worked for Amrish all day long. In three years he was able to obtain traditional financing and pay off the higher-interest loan. Additionally, his building equity grew as the real estate market climbed in his favor.

Property Qualification

You have a building under contract and have selected a lender. The required financials have been submitted for approval. But you are only halfway to the finish line. The next step is for the bank to qualify the property. View this part of the process as an interested third party whose goal is to assure you succeed in business by investigating the property thoroughly. Here is what lenders investigate:

- **Appraisal:** Lenders require a property appraisal before approving a loan to determine the property value and calculate its loan-to-value ratio. A commercial appraisal report can take between two and four weeks. Depending on the size of the building, this may cost $2,500.
- **ALTA Survey**: An ALTA survey safeguards your investment from critical discrepancies that a simple title search or basic survey may not disclose, such as building encroachments or utility easements on your property. Knowing this information lowers the risk for

you as the future owner. The survey can take between two and four weeks and costs about $2,500 to $5,000.

- **Phase I / Environmental Report:** As mentioned in chapter five, "You're Not Buying a Home," the Phase I report is an explorative report that digs into the property's history, along with a site visit to determine if further investigation is required relating to environmentally hazardous materials. The report assesses the likelihood of impurities on the site, such as lead, oil, and/or toxic chemicals. It typically takes between two and four weeks to complete a Phase I site assessment. Again, it costs around $2,500, more if a Phase II or III report is required. Chapter Five has additional information on Phase I, II, and III requirements.

The appraisal, Phase I, and ALTA survey reports are sent to the lender's team for review and consent prior to the buyer receiving final financing approval. If the Phase I requires further investigation, the property sale will be on hold until the investigation is complete, and the property has a clean bill of health. If the ALTA survey shows an encroachment within the property boundaries, this needs to be resolved prior to closing.

Business Tip: The due diligence period is another negotiating opportunity for the buyer. Depending on what the building inspection and the appraisal reveal, this may present a chance to renegotiate the purchase price and receive a buyer credit at the close of escrow to compensate for a lower appraisal price or major building repairs.

The appraisal needs to match the purchase price or be higher for the lender to fund the approved loan. If the appraisal is lower than the agreed upon purchase price, negotiations between seller and buyer begin again, delicately. The seller and buyer have a few options:

1. The buyer can cancel escrow and have the earnest monies refunded.

2. The buyer can pay out of pocket the difference between the appraised value and the agreed upon price.

3. The seller can pay the difference between appraised value and agreed upon price.

4. Seller and buyer can split the difference between appraised value and agreed upon price.

5. The appraisal can be contested, but chances of a valuation change is rare.

Purchasing commercial real estate property or expanding existing property is often a major commitment, and these requirements from your lender can be costly. To offset the pain of these upfront costs, ask the lender to roll them into the loan at closing.

Office Condo Inspections Differ from Fee Simple Properties

An office condominium requires a different inspection process. A lender will generally rely on the plat map over a survey, which is recommended for a fee simple property. A plat map shows the lender how the tract of land is divided into lots. Typically, a building owner owns the land below the building. All other land and easements are owned by the association. The building owner shares the cost in their prorate share of ownership within the complex. Furthermore, it will show streets, rights of way, flood zones, boundaries, and the size of your building. The lender will reference the plat map to confirm the unit's recorded size and boundaries.

In addition to a plat map, a lender may ask for an environmental questionnaire from the seller instead of a Phase I report. The questionnaire screens for potential environmental hazards on the property and involves the seller answering questions to the best of their knowledge. This involves less time and money than a Phase I report.

The Importance of the Right Lender

Greg and his partner, Sam, dreamed they could buy an office condo for their new law firm. Their lease expired in two months, with no opportunity to extend. They had recently broken off from a prestigious law firm and had fifteen years of litigation experience, but only a year in their new venture. This was the perfect time to buy a building.

It would be a challenge to connect this buyer with a lender that could approve a new business run by experienced lawyers and close the deal in less than two months. There was minimal chance to succeed within traditional lending timelines.

Before touring properties, the law firm was introduced to a young loan officer, Drew, who worked at a mid-size local bank. Drew had proved himself in the past, yet this was a new test for him. Drew immediately sent his financial request list to the buyers, and the lawyers turned around the information quickly.

But could the perfect office be located, negotiated, purchase contract signed, and inspections completed for the buyer and the lender within two months?

After a month of searching, Greg and Sam found the right fit for their budding business. But with only a month left on their lease, could the team close the sale?

The buyer's rep asked Drew the question of the day. "Drew, we found the right property yet, due to Sam and Greg's existing lease terms, we only have thirty days to close. The landlord has denied their request for a short lease extension. Can you get the sale closed in time?"

Drew responded, "If the buyer is willing to pay for expedited reports, I believe we can, but we have to jump on it right now. I just received word from underwriting that we only need one additional piece of information to get them officially approved. And, of course, the inspections need to support the purchase."

Drew accomplished a mini miracle and closed the property a few days early. Everyone breathed a sigh of relief. Having a competent buyer's rep and an innovative go-getter lender can move things in a timely manner.

The next phase, step seven, is part of the due diligence period that involves the practicality of remodeling. It examines if the real estate supports the buyer's vision through space planning, an estimated construction cost, and how long it will take to complete the renovation.

STEP SEVEN
Redesign and Construction

Keywords: move-in ready, turn-key, second generation, shell space, build-to-suit, architect, customize, space plan, CAD drawing, license/bonded contractor, cost engineered, contractor, scope of work, preliminary bid, actual bid, bid summary, cost engineer, soft costs, timeline, project manager

Timeline:

Architecture: *One to two weeks in a slow market. Three to four weeks in a high-demand market.*

Construction: *Depends on the remodel. It can be one to nine months. Anticipate another few months in a steamy hot market.*

Lifeline Insurance has selected its new location. Now, the real work begins. It is time to personalize the office suite to fit the company culture. Ideally, the cost to complete the remodel is analyzed prior to the expiration of Dan's due diligence period. The cost for Lifeline Insurance to modify its new building is minimal, yet other buyers will start from a blank slate. Designing the office requires a space planner, architect and/or interior designer, depending on the suite's condition prior to move-in, and a reasonable timeframe. A lender often wraps these soft costs for remodeling into the mortgage. This is another reason to establish your Tenant Improvement (TI) costs during your Due Diligence (DD) period.

Prior to detailing buyer improvements and customizing the building, it is important to understand the different kinds of office space.

1. *Move-in ready space.*

2. *Second generation space.*

3. *Shell space.*

Move-in Ready

A move-in ready suite is ideal for a buyer with a short time frame. It does not require buyer improvements. A property in this condition meets the buyer's specific needs, all city or governing municipality requirements, and is habitable for immediate use. The buyer can relocate to move-in ready space once the property closes.

Business Owner Tip: If a buyer needs an office space in less than sixty days, target move-in ready properties.

Second Generation Space

Lifeline's new office space is considered *second generation* space—a building previously occupied by another buyer. Dan plans on doing some renovations to the property, and this will require additional funds. His lender will "roll" the renovation costs into the loan, making it part of the monthly payment. Another choice for Dan is to pay cash for the improvements.

Dan wants to lender finance the improvements. For this to happen, the lender insists the remodel cost be defined prior to closing on the property. Dan must submit a bid from a licensed and bonded contractor. Amanda, Dan's buyer rep, strongly suggests that Dan get two or more construction bids from reputable contractors *before* the end of his due diligence period. This way Dan and his lender clearly understand the remodel cost and timing.

Business Owner Tip: When securing more than one construction bid, it is courteous to inform the other contractors.

Shell Space

A new office building constructed without specific buyers in mind is called a spec office building or shell space. Developers take a calculated risk based on location, demand, and market conditions. The developer constructs the building for a future user. The space is enclosed by an exterior building shell, yet the interior remains a blank slate aside from electrical, plumbing, and mechanical fixtures. If it is a multi-story shell building, elevators and stairwells are installed. This enables the buyer to customize the building based on their individual requirements.

A buyer should allow six to nine months to complete the shell space. The six to nine month timeframe starts from opening escrow and includes space planning, architectural drawings, and construction.

$$$ Saving Tip: When buying a completed shell space, aim for the closing date to coincide with the completion of your architectural drawings and building permits approved from the city. This way, you have less time to pay your loan before occupying the space. Lenders often allow the buyer to pay interest only during the buildout phase.

Customize Your Office Space

Prior to the end of the due diligence period, the buyer needs to design the office, estimate the cost within 5 to 10 percent, and determine if they will finance the remodel or pay cash. For Lifeline Insurance, the space is configured close to what Dan wants, so there is a clear idea of what modifications are required.

The buyer, with or without the assistance of the buyer rep, coordinates and manages the necessary professionals to build out the space. The buyer should always hire licensed, bonded professionals. *Licensed* means the contractor has passed city requirements for commercial construction. *Bonded* provides the buyer an avenue to recoup losses if the job is done poorly.

Floor Plan Development Example

The first step in estimating construction costs is to have a space planner, draftsman, or architect design the office space. This must be done before soliciting contractors for bids, as the floor plan may require multiple revisions.

SIMPLY OWN IT!

Had Lifeline Insurance needed substantial suite revisions, Dan and his team, or the buyer rep, would have outlined what they needed and sent the requirement to a space planner or architect.

Below is an existing floor plan of a poorly designed office that an advertising group wanted to buy. The ad group asked the space planner to modernize the space. They did not need a reception area, only four offices with windows and a breakroom/lounge area. A computer generated architectural *CAD* drawing is created rather simply once parameters are defined.

Industry Lingo: Computer-aided design, *CAD*, is software used by architects, engineers, and drafters to create a 2D floor plan design for contractors to build from.

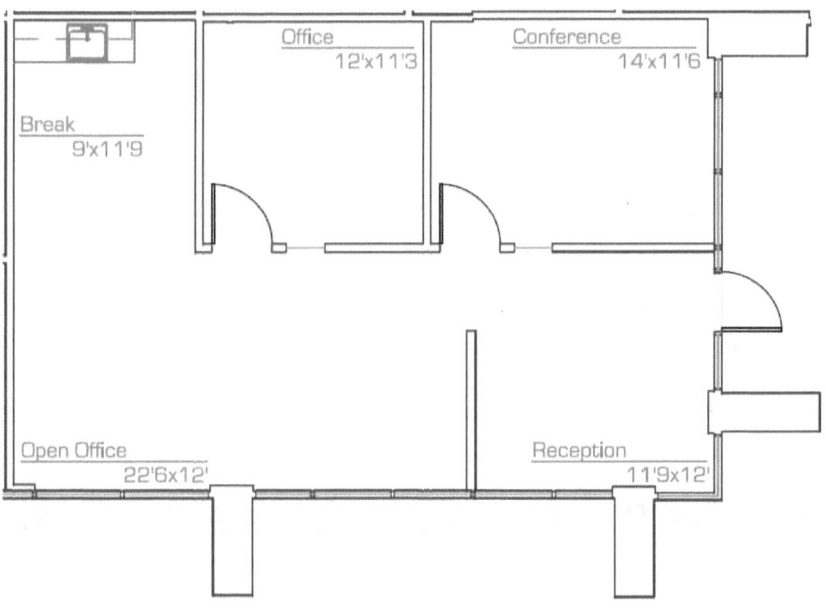

The advertising group reviewed the architects efficiently laid out drawing and requested the storage be incorporated into the cabinet area. Afterwards, all parties met on site to solidify the floor plan. Often there are multiple revisions before a floor plan is approved.

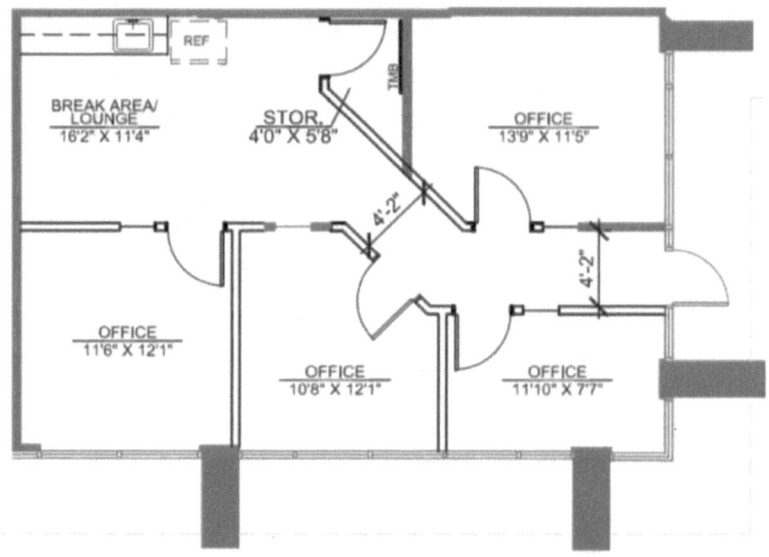

$$$ Saving Tip: Prior to finalizing a floor plan, meet on location with professionals when redesigning space and assessing costs. Discoveries can be made that will save money during reconstruction.

Remodeling Preparation Coordinated by the Buyer Rep

Buyer reps are an invaluable resource of information. They can easily recommend qualified and reliable professionals for the buyer to work with to determine the actual improvement costs. Once the space plan is approved it can be sent to contractors to write an estimated bid on the scope of work. Usually, this estimate with a 10 to 15 percent fudge factor is adequate for the underwriter to approve the extra financing cost. For a more accurate bid from a contractor, a complete set of architectural drawings are required.

$$$ Saving Tip: If possible, prior to the expiration of the due diligence period, ask for actual construction costs versus an estimate bid. If the remodel is an excessive cost, the buyer can cancel escrow and receive a refund for his earnest monies.

Buyer Remodel Action Plan

The buyer and lender have signed off on the renovation. Ideally, this happens before the buyer's due diligence period ends. Additionally, the buyer examines budgeting costs and remodel timing. Remodel notes help all parties be on the same page and understand the scope of work prior to bidding the project.

Business Owner Tip: Avoid using a handyman to cut corners. Most municipalities require the use of licensed/bonded contractors for commercial construction. This provides protection if something goes awry during construction.

To determine costs, the buyer forwards the agreed-upon floor plan and remodel notes to select contractors to bid the scope of work. Renovation costs can be *cost engineered*, or revised, to bring the costs within budget and manage cost expectations.

Contractor Preliminary Bids

When bidding a construction project, the contractor tours the suite, reviews the floor plan, consults subcontractors, and then offers a preliminary bid to the buyer. It is best to obtain three or more contractor bids to provide a strong idea of the potential buildout cost. My first three office condo bids came in so high, I found two other companies to bid the job. Ultimately it saved me $200,000.

Preliminary bids are based on the approved floor plan, which do not include drawings for mechanical, plumbing, and structural engineering. It is too costly. The preliminary bid is an educated estimate. An experienced contractor is usually within 10 percent of the actual cost of the buildout.

The building owner can now compare the bids side-by-side to make sure the line items for the work are comparable. These preliminary numbers provide a buyer with a ballpark figure to budget for the new buildout. If the renovation cost is higher than expected, the buyer can change the floor plan or the finishes to reduce expenses. It is a professional courtesy to avoid discussing one contractor's bid with another contractor.

The best-case scenario is to have actual costs of the buildout prior to closing on the property and ask the contractor for a guaranteed bid if you have architectural and engineering drawings approved.

Actual Buildout Cost

Actual construction costs are refined once the buyer does their homework and is confident this is the right building to buy. This justifies the significant cost for a complete set of architectural drawings, including plumbing, electrical, and mechanical drawings. Flooring and finishes for the suite should be selected if they haven't already. This process takes about three months. It may or may not be completed prior to a finalized sale.

My office condo remodel started in early 2021 while city officials were working from home. This delayed my architectural timeline by a month.

The initial submission of plans and the second review took over four months. So, depending on world affairs, budget your time accordingly.

Typically, the lowest bidder wins the contract to remodel the property. However, this may vary depending on a contractor's reputation and availability to complete the job before the buyer's move-in date. The lowest bidder may be backlogged with work orders and not able to start your project in a timely manner.

After getting over sticker shock on the buildout cost of my new office, we chose to wait one month for our preferred contractor, Billy. "I'd love to do the job, but I won't take it on until I complete some of my other commitments that are delayed because of backed up orders," he said. "I understand if you need to choose another contractor." His sincerity sealed the deal, along with his pricing and the quality of his work.

When the remodel cost is higher than expected, review your company's priorities. One area to reconsider is cabinetry, one of the costlier components of a buildout. Discuss alternative solutions, such as furniture.

Handcrafted millwork for my condo was quoted at $60,000. I mentioned this at our furniture meeting and our furniture rep said that his company could order us cabinets to match the furniture. When I let go of my idea of natural wood only, he calculated the cost at $45,000. Additionally, because the cabinets were now classified as furniture by the IRS, 75 percent of the cost would be depreciated over one year versus five years.

Contractor Bid Summary Example

Lifeline has three reputable contractors bid the office buildout. Some of the line items vary substantially, such as plumbing, electrical, and ceiling. The three bids range from $88,572 to $105,228. This is a wide variance and requires further exploration from Dan.

DESCRIPTION	Integrity Building			Build Strategic			CR Commercial		
	Standard	Non Standard	Cost/USF	Standard	Non Standard	Cost/USF	Standard	Non Standard	Cost/USF
Calendar Days									
Demolition	$ 3,280.00		$ 1.54	$ 3,800.00		$ 1.79	$ 3,200.00		$ 1.51
Concrete (including termite pretreat)	$ 240.00		$ 0.11			$ -			$ -
Roof and / or Slab Penetrations						$ -			$ -
Rough Carpentry	$ 265.00		$ 0.12			$ -	$ 770.00		$ 0.36
Finish Carpentry						$ -			$ -
Millwork	$ 11,136.00		$ 5.24	$ 15,183.82		$ 7.15	$ 11,400.00		$ 5.37
Insulation	$ 810.00		$ 0.38	$ 610.00		$ 0.29	$ 667.00		$ 0.31
Doors, Frames, and Hardware	$ 3,536.00		$ 1.66	$ 2,700.00		$ 1.27	$ 3,150.00		$ 1.48
Glass and Glazing			$ -	$ 460.80		$ 0.22	$ 1,227.00		$ 0.58
Drywall and Metal Stud Framing	$ 11,882.00		$ 5.59	$ 11,675.00		$ 5.50	$ 8,510.00		$ 4.01
Acoustical Ceiling Tile / Grid	$ 4,384.00		$ 2.06	$ 5,679.00		$ 2.67	$ 4,250.00		$ 2.00
Floor Covering	$ 22,680.00		$ 10.68	$ 23,026.36		$ 10.84	$ 22,505.00		$ 10.60
Ceramic Tile or Stone			$ -			$ -			$ -
Carpet			$ -			$ -			$ -
VCT			$ -			$ -			$ -
Carpet/Rubber Base			$ -			$ -			$ -
VCT Seal and Wax			$ -			$ -			$ -
Painting and Wallcovering	$ 3,304.00		$ 1.56	$ 2,793.00		$ 1.31	$ 3,300.00		$ 1.55
Fire Extinguishers			$ -			$ -			$ -
Toilet Accessories, Partitions and FR	$ 500.00		$ 0.24	$ 540.00		$ 0.25			$ -
Window Treatments / Blinds			$ -			$ -			$ -
Plumbing	$ 16,105.00		$ 7.56	$ 15,403.00		$ 7.25	$ 11,550.00		$ 5.44
Fire Protection / Sprinkler	$ 2,174.00		$ 1.02	$ 1,108.00		$ 0.52	$ 1,255.00		$ 0.59
HVAC / Mechanical / Ductwork	$ 10,622.00		$ 5.00	$ 10,775.00		$ 5.07	$ 8,500.00		$ 4.00
Electrical	$ 16,853.00		$ 7.93	$ 17,401.90		$ 8.19	$ 17,600.00		$ 8.29
Fire Alarm	$ 3,320.00		$ 1.56	$ 3,320.00		$ 1.56	$ 3,387.00		$ 1.59
EMS Sytems	$ 1,697.00		$ 0.80	$ 1,697.00		$ 0.80	$ 1,697.00		$ 0.80
Other			$ -			$ -			$ -
Other			$ -			$ -			$ -
General Conditions	$ 20,442.00		$ 9.62	$ 8,480.80		$ 3.99	$ 5,371.00		$ 2.53
Overhead & Profit	$ 9,392.00		$ 4.42	$ 8,351.80		$ 3.93	$ 5,468.95		$ 2.57
Insurance-Builder's Risk Coverage	$ 1,413.00		$ 0.67			$ -	$ 548.70		$ 0.26
Sales Tax			$ -			$ -	$ 3,907.00		$ 1.84
Alternates Included in Total									
Vinyl plank flooring ILO ceramic tile (except rest rooms)			$ -			$ -	$ (11,736.00)		$ (5.53)
Delete washer / dryer hook-ups			$ -			$ -	$ (1,500.00)		$ (0.71)
Use white toilets / sinks ILO black			$ -			$ -	$ (1,250.00)		$ (0.59)
Delete (2) 220v circuits			$ -			$ -	$ (1,000.00)		$ (0.47)
HVAC redesign - use more of exiting ductwork			$ -			$ -	$ (3,000.00)		$ (1.41)
Landlord's share of permitting costs			$ -			$ -	$ (3,731.00)		$ (1.76)
SUBTOTAL CONTRACT AMOUNT	$ 144,035.00	$0.00	$ 67.61	$ 133,005.48	$0.00	$ 62.62	$ 96,042.65	$0.00	$ 45.22

DESCRIPTION	Integrity Building			Build Strategic			JDI Development		
	Standard	Non Standard	Cost/USF	Standard	Non standard	Cost/USF	Standard	Non standard	Cost/USF
SUBTOTAL CONTRACT AMOUNT	$ 92,013.00	$0.00	$ 43.32	$ 105,228.10	$0.00	$ 49.54	$ 88,572.80	$0.00	$ 41.70
TOTAL GC'S CONTRACT AMOUNT	$92,013.00		$ 43.32	$105,228.10		$ 49.54	$88,572.80		$ 41.70
Alternates NIC in Total									
			$ -			$ -			$ -
			$ -			$ -			$ -
	$ -		$ -	$		$ -	$		$ -

Soft Costs

Contractors' bids include the cost of construction, or hard costs. You'll also need to budget for soft costs, which include space planning, architectural and engineering costs, and permits and construction fees. These can total over ten dollars per square foot. If they are not anticipated or included when presenting the initial renovation costs to the lender, a buyer will be caught off guard with unanticipated expenditures after the closing.

In the example below, soft costs total over $20,000 for 2,100 square feet, the equivalent of $10.30 per square foot. These costs, easily overlooked when one focuses only on construction prices, eat into a buyer's reserve fund.

Soft Cost Examples

Soft Costs	Costs	Cost / SF
Space Planning	$1,250.00	$0.59
Asbestos Inspection Fee	$900.00	$0.42
Construction Documents (CD)	$10,475.00	$4.93
Architectural Reimbursable	$500.00	$0.24
Plan Check Fee (allowance)	$1,500.00	$0.71
Permit Fee (allowance)	$5,259.89	$2.48
Total Soft Costs	**$21,884.89**	**$10.30**

Can you imagine how angry Dan will be if he finds out he has to pay these costs in addition to his loan on a 10,500 square foot building? So much for the great interest rates that were negotiated earlier. In Lifeline's deal, an oversight of this magnitude would cost Dan $108,000 out of pocket.

With all remodel costs accounted for, the buyer can make an educated decision. Dan prefers to hold his cash for business growth and new hires; thus, he calls his lender and asks for a revised term sheet to include the remodel. Satisfied with the construction bids and timeline, Dan checks one more box on his due diligence list and waits for the lenders updated mortgage numbers. Dan is in the final phase of his purchase as he advances to step eight, the close.

Post-Closing Construction

The remodel starts once the property has closed escrow and the title is transferred to the buyer's name. The construction time varies, yet on an average the buyer can budget one to three months for a facelift to the property.

Understand that unforeseen variables can extend the construction timeline and plan accordingly. The contractor and I budgeted four months for my complete office condo renovation, and it was seven months later when I moved in. As I mentioned in the opening of the book, when I started construction, the US was experiencing labor shortages as well as supply chain interruptions.

Certificate of Occupancy

Once construction is completed and the building passes final city inspections, the property owner receives a Final Certificate of Occupancy (C of O) from the city. If an owner needs to move in before a final city inspection, a Temporary Certificate of Occupancy *may* be issued. This temporary certificate allows an owner to occupy the building until the buildout is completed.

In addition to receiving your C of O, confirm the contractor and the subcontractors have released all construction liens on the property. You do not want an unwarranted construction lien becoming an encumbrance on your title report.

STEP EIGHT

The Home Stretch, the Close

Keywords: due diligence approval, closing, settlement statement,

Timeline: *fifteen to sixty days or as defined in the PSA*

Once you've checked off everything on the to-do list during your due diligence period, you are in the home stretch and ready to close on the property. But first, let's double check the inspection period and make sure the buyer is ready to release their earnest monies and move forward.

Below is a checklist for your due diligence review:

1. Any documents the seller provides the buyer.

    a. Conditions, Covenants, and Restrictions (CC&R's) for the condominium.

    b. Architectural drawings.

     c.   Parking information.

     d.   Building reports from repairs.

     e.   Statement from insurance provider regarding any potential claims.

     f.   Electric bills, service contracts, property taxes, etc.

2. Financing approval.

3. Building inspections.

     a.   General building inspection.

     b.   Termite inspection.

     c.   Sewer cam report to see the condition of the sewer lines.

4. Environmental questionnaire or Phase I report.

5. Appraisal.

6. Remodel estimated cost.

7. ALTA survey.

8. Title commitment report, and especially the Schedule B.

9. Tenant lease (if there is a tenant occupying a portion of the building).

Attorney Value

A local commercial real estate attorney offers deeper legal perspective than that of a broker when buying a building. They are that third eye, assisting with the purchase transaction and the closing process with your interest at heart. The attorney often identifies challenges your buyer rep is not aware of because it falls outside of the rep's scope of expertise.

Dan's attorney, James, reviews the Schedule B and notices a construction lien that lingers from the previous owner's buildout. The seller has documentation proving the bill has been paid and the lien is satisfied. For James, with his knowledge of how the system works, this is an easy fix. The title officer omits the lien from the Schedule B, and the property is ready to close. The broker, Amanda, would have been at a loss in the legal arena.

Due Diligence Review Approval

Dan, Amanda, and James review all the feasibility materials and collectively decide that this is the building for Dan. With all the due diligence items satisfied, Dan decides to move forward with the purchase and the earnest monies became non-refundable. The funds remain in escrow and will be debited from the purchase price on the buyer's side of the settlement statement.

Escrow Cancelation

If Dan had found a significant problem that could not be resolved and decided to cancel escrow, he would have needed to notify the title company in writing before the expiration of the due diligence period. Email suffices and should state that he elects to cancel escrow and demands the refund of his earnest monies in full, per the contract, Section such and such. The title company passes the notice on to the seller and all related parties in the transaction. If the seller agrees, he/she signs a release form from the title company and returns the document. The monies are deposited back in Dan's account. This may take a day or two to come full cycle.

Seller Refuses to Accept the Cancelation Demand

If the seller refuses to release the earnest monies for any reason, the money is held in escrow until there is a resolution. In a dispute like this, attorneys are engaged to interpret the intent of the contract language. It is rare to have these disputes, but when they arise, real estate attorneys are well trained to resolve issues.

Cruise Control

Once the homework phase is over and a buyer has approved financing, the tough time-consuming examination process is done. Usually, the buyer has fifteen to thirty days after due diligence expiration to close on the building. During this period, the lender is completing the loan docs and the title company and/or attorney are tidying up any title objections and preparing the closing papers. The buyer can sit back and enjoy the ride for a few weeks until examination of legal documents is required.

Closing Process

About two weeks prior to the closing date, the title company will send out a list of last-minute items seller and buyer need to satisfy for the property to close. Every deal is different and has different closing checklists. Some documents require notarization, while others can be signed electronically.

A seller's closing checklist includes the following items and more:

1. Proof of property tax payment or lack thereof.
2. Payoff statement for any outstanding fees.
3. Seller settlement statement approval.
4. Legal description of property.
5. Owner's affidavit—commercial. (The owner's affidavit states that the seller owned the property, free and clear of liens and/or non-recorded easements.)
6. Affidavit of No Open Deeds of Trust or Mortgage(s)

A buyer's closing checklist includes the following and more:

1. Operating agreement for the LLC that was created to purchase the building.
2. Lender contact information for building pay off.
3. Buyer settlement statement approval.

SIMPLY OWN IT!

Settlement Statement Example

Stewart Title & Trust of Phoenix, Inc.
2930 E Camelback Rd., Ste 210
Phoenix, AZ 85016
(602) 462-8000

COMBINED FINAL CLOSING STATEMENT

File Number:	1289804
Loan Amount:	$372,810.00
Sales Price:	$438,600.00
Close Date:	8/30/2021
Disbursement Date:	8/30/2021

Property: 8160 EAST BUTHERUS DRIVE, UNIT #5
SCOTTSDALE, AZ 85260 (MARICOPA)
(215-55-062)

Certified True and Correct Copy

Stewart Title & Trust of Phoenix, Inc.

Buyer(s): MANTA PROPERTIES LLC, AN ARIZONA LIMITED LIABILITY COMPANY
8160 East Butherus Drive
Unit #5
Scottsdale, AZ 85260

Seller(s): STUART J. SPIVAK
8160 East Butherus Drive
Unit #5
Scottsdale, AZ 85260

Description	Buyer Debit	Buyer Credit		Seller Debit	Seller Credit
Deposits, Credits, Debits					
Contract sales price	$438,600.00				$438,600.00
Deposit or Earnest Money		$20,000.00			
Closing funds from (DISABLED) Healing Wounds, LLC, an Arizona limited liability company		$46,909.76			
Earnest money retained by					
Disbursed as proceeds ($20,000.00)					
Prorations					
County taxes 7/1/2021 to 9/30/2021 @ $1,533.68/Six Months		$807.96		$807.96	
Commissions					
$20,000.00 to Andrea Davis CRE					
to					
Commission paid at Settlement				$20,000.00	
New Loans					
Principal amount of new loan		$372,810.00			
Appraisal Fee to (NA) First-Citizens Bank & Trust (POC $1,150.00 by Borrower)					
Commitment Fee to (NA) First-Citizens Bank & Trust (POC $3,588.00 by Borrower)					
Flood Research Fee to (NA) First-Citizens Bank & Trust (POC $6.00 by Borrower)					
Environmental Fee to (NA) First-Citizens Bank & Trust (POC $305.00 by Borrower)					
Title Charges					
Lender's coverage $372,810.00 Premium $100.00 to Stewart Title & Trust of Phoenix, Inc.	$100.00				
Owner's coverage $438,600.00 Premium $1,893.00 to Stewart Title & Trust of Phoenix, Inc.	$631.00			$1,262.00	
ALTA 4-06 Condominium 2-3-10 (Issued With Policy) Endorsement(s) to Stewart Title & Trust of Phoenix, Inc.	$75.00				
ALTA 8.2-06 Commercial Environmental Protections Lien 10-16-08 Endorsement(s) to Stewart Title & Trust of Phoenix, Inc.	$100.00				
ALTA 9-06 Restrictions, Encroachments, Minerals-Loan Policy 4-2-12 (Issued With Endorsement(s) to Stewart Title & Trust of Phoenix, Inc.					
Settlement or closing fee to Stewart Title & Trust of Phoenix, Inc.	$665.50			$665.50	
Notary fees to Stewart Title & Trust of Phoenix, Inc.				$150.00	
Government Recording and Transfer Charges					
Recording fees: Deed $30.00				$30.00	
Mortgage $30.00	$30.00				
Additional Settlement Charges					
Property Tax Due all 2021 1st half to Maricopa County Treasurer				$1,533.68	
Association Dues - August to (NA) Belvedere Office Association (POC $475.00 by Stuart J. Spivak)					
Association Dues - Sept Dues to (NA) Belvedere Office Association				$475.00	
Totals	$440,262.50	$440,527.74		$25,025.14	$438,600.00

Balance Due TO Buyer: $275.24   Balance Due TO Seller: $413,574.86

Approve the Settlement Statement

When reviewing the settlement statement, double-check all line items. If you find a potential discrepancy, inform the title company, and they will adjust the sum accordingly. Areas that are often miscalculated include:

1. Property taxes need to be properly prorated between seller and buyer.

2. If the property has an association, assure the HOA fees are prorated correctly between seller and buyer based on when the seller last paid them.

3. If there is a tenant, check the lease to find out if the seller is holding a security deposit for the tenant. This will be a debit for the seller and a credit for the buyer.

4. If there is a tenant and the rent is paid in advance, confirm the rent is prorated between seller and buyer.

5. Verify all fees charged to the buyer.

When all parties agree to the settlement statement numbers, the closing will take place within a few days.

Congratulations on Your NEW Building!

Once closed, the property transfers title into the buyer's name after the deed is officially recorded. The title company will send a congratulatory email with the following official documents. A combined signed settlement statement.

6. A special warranty deed, the recorded deed that is signed by the seller and notarized.

7. A deed of trust signed by the buyer and notarized.

8. When a lease is involved, an executed and notarized assignment of rents.

SIMPLY OWN IT!

While these documents are public record, it is advisable to keep them in a safe file, along with your due diligence reports. Keys will be turned over at the closing table or hand delivered. Your tenant rep can coordinate the key relay.

As the new owner, now is the time to engage your contractor and other vendors necessary to assist with your move. Step nine outlines the move-in process.

STEP NINE
Ownership, One Task at a Time

Keywords: IT, phone, security, audio visual, limited liability insurance, leaseback, certificate of insurance

Timeline: *Without renovations, one to two weeks. With renovations, up to six months.*

Your move-in day is almost here. You've interviewed and selected your buyer rep, found the property, and are about to close. The plans for buildout are ready to execute. Pat yourself on the back for getting this far. There are a few more items on the checklist before you move in.

Getting and Staying Connected

Prior to closing and while the remodel is underway, you can line up your vendors, such as IT professionals, audio-visual professionals, security providers, utility supplier, phones, new furniture, and a mover. Often your

IT, phone, and security vendor will need to coordinate running wires as the suite is being built out.

The mover can be scheduled when the project is almost done and there is an actual completion date.

Timing of these projects is like a choreographed dance scene. Moving in early without flooring or paint will be like moving twice. Audio visual tools are the link to successful interactions with prospects and customers. Without connectivity, your business is on hold.

Wi-Fi connectivity posed another weeklong delay for my office condo move in. I assumed incorrectly that my IT provider would call our local provider, Cox Communications, to turn on the switch. By time I got around to it, Cox would not just flip the "on" switch because there had been no Wi-Fi at this location for over four years. "Live and learn" is what my mother always says in situations like this. At this point, I needed to roll with the punches and take another fictitious chill pill.

Additional Closing Odds and Ends

Leaseback from the Building LLC

Leasebacks can provide tax benefits for companies. One reason companies buy a building is for tax benefits. To maximize tax benefits, your company can lease office space from the building LLC. The building LLC technically becomes the landlord, and an actual lease needs to be signed between the parties. If you are financing the purchase, your lender may require an in-place lease as part of the lending requirements. Check with your CPA and financial planner for the most advantageous way to maximize your tax benefits.

Limited Liability Insurance

One can never be too careful. Landlords require tenants to purchase limited liability insurance prior to move-in, and the specifics are spelled out in the lease. As a new building owner and landlord, the lease you set up between your company and the building LLC should require limited liability insurance. The amount of insurance varies depending on the amount of coverage you want. Ask your insurance agent for guidance on the best limited liability insurance for your company.

An example of lease language requiring insurance:

Section 4.04. Insurance Policies

(a) Liability Insurance. During the Lease Term, Tenant shall maintain a policy of commercial general liability insurance (sometimes known as broad form comprehensive general liability insurance) insuring Tenant against liability for bodily injury, property damage (including loss of use of property), and personal injury arising out of the operation, use, or occupancy of the Property. Tenant shall name Landlord and Landlord's property management company as additional insureds under such policy. The initial amount of such insurance shall be Two Million Dollars ($2,000,000) per occurrence and shall be subject to periodic increase based upon inflation, increased liability awards, recommendation of Landlord's professional insurance advisers, and other relevant factors.

Upon securing limited liability insurance, the insurance agent will issue a certificate of insurance for your records. It summarizes key aspects and conditions of the policy.

You did it!

Congratulations! It's time to set aside any relocation stress and enjoy the fruits of your labor. A new office is inspirational, an opportunity to throw out baggage and bring in the new. Ownership supports the foundation of your dreams from the ground up. Clients and patients vicariously enjoy the vibe of your new environment, and your business reflects your persistent work.

In case you forget why you purchased, here are a few of the top reasons.

- Pride of ownership.
- Stabilized mortgage payments.
- Strengthened retirement plan when you choose to sell or lease the property.
- Equity in the property.
- Additional tax benefits.
- You are your own landlord.
- Control your destiny.
- The American dream!

Enjoy the rewards of property ownership. You earned it!

EPILOGUE
Well … that was fun. Exiting Your Business

Keywords: business expansion, consolidation, business sale, leaseback, 1031 tax deferred exchange

Time to Sell?

Time passes quickly, and that new building purchase benefited your company for quite a while. The time has come to exit stage left. Selling, leasing, vacating, or doing a sale-leaseback differ for each business. There are so many reasons to change locations, and some may involve the following.

1. **Business expansion.** Dave and Derek, tax attorneys, searched long and hard for an office condo that would provide room for growth over the next five years. To their surprise, within one year, business soared, and they outgrew their office. They

167

needed to hire additional attorneys and find an office twice as large. Their buyer rep shared first-hand knowledge about current market conditions for a new office. Additionally, they strategized on what to do with their current office—sell or lease?

2. **Change in business direction.** After fifteen years of growth, Greg's logistics business hit a peak, or so he thought. He owned a large warehouse that was 100 percent air conditioned, which was needed to support the product he stored for his primary pharmaceutical client. To justify the purchase, Greg moved his corporate office into the property. Two years later the pharmaceutical client merged with a larger company, and the contract was dissolved. During those two years, Greg secured several other large clients who needed traditional warehouse storage. He sold the non-traditional corporate office with a generous profit and purchased a warehouse and distribution center three times the size that supported the logistics company's new business direction. To defer capital gains, he exercised a 1031 tax deferred exchange.

3. **Retirement is imminent.** Dr. Arora, an ophthalmologist, originally bought his office condo so that when he retired, he could cash out and buy a home in the mountains. A few years prior to retiring, his business neighbors were clamoring about record sale prices within his office condo project. He decided to capitalize on the seller's market and keep practicing for five more years before moving. His buyer rep suggested

a sale-leaseback, where Dr. Arora could stay in the property for five years after selling the property as an investment to a new owner who would capture the rental income. Investments such as a sale-leaseback are complex and could fill a book. A specialized commercial real estate expert can guide you through the detailed process.

4. **The business consolidated.** As technology progresses, it allows some business to run more efficiently with less physical space. When a business downsizes, it makes economic sense to sell the property or lease out a portion to offset expenses. Diane's business was growing, yet fewer employees were needed at the office. With half of the office vacant, she decided to split the office and generate income. She could still control her destiny, sell when it fit her exit timing, and know that if her business grew, additional space was available.

5. **Your business sold, so now what?** You own your building, and it is advantageous to sell your business. What are your options?

   When you sell your business to someone who wants to continue it in its current location, you can lease or sell the property you own to the new business owner.

   Dr. Hwang purchased his own building because a surgery center costs an exorbitant amount to build out. He decided to invest in his own building, not a landlord's. Additionally, he strategized that in ten to fifteen years he would sell his business, lease the building to the new business owner, and enjoy a monthly rental income. He accomplished his goal quicker than antici-pated and repeated the process three times within the ten-year plan.

Business Owner Tip: Buying a building, positioning the business for sale, and leasing the building to the new owner requires a cohesive team. Make sure you include your buyer rep as part of the team from the start.

6. **The company needs a cash infusion.** Not all acquisi-tions end up a bowl full of Cheerios. Marion's business plan shifted from a classic physical therapy office to one that scientifically trains professional athletes using high-tech workouts and herbal supplements. She owned her PT office location yet found the train-ing business required a warehouse component and a lot of start-up cash. Instead of finding an investor to expand the business, Marion opted to sell her office and lease warehouse space until she had historical data to support another purchase. Since it was a seller's market, Marion sold with enough equity to invest in the new business instead of seeking outside funds.

Whatever reason a business owner chooses to sell his property, he or she should consult with a qualified local commercial broker and attorney who specializes in their product type. For example, if you are selling an office condo or a fee simple office property, engage a commercial real estate office broker, and do the same if it is a retail or industrial building. Plan on six to twelve months to sell your commercial asset. This wide range of time depends on your financial expectations, if it is a seller's market or a buyer's market, amount of inventory, and the complexity of the transaction.

When listing a property for sale follow this guideline:

1. Broker Selection: interviews may take you one to two weeks. Look for compatibility and someone who genuinely cares about your business.

2. Marketing: two to four weeks to prepare the marketing materials to go live with the listing.

3. Property tours and offers to buy: this can take up to six months or more.

4. LOI & contract negotiations: four to six weeks.

5. Average due diligence: sixty to ninety days.

6. Average closing time: 15-60 days

7. From the time you decide to sell until funds are transferred can take 6-12 months, so plan accordingly.

1031 Tax Deferred Exchange

Before closing on your property, decide if you want to take advantage of a 1031 tax deferred exchange. U.S. Internal Revenue Code Section 1031 allows the deferral of capital gains taxes on the sale of property held for investment or productive use in a trade or a business. With a 1031 exchange, property owners can sell their real estate, and then reinvest the proceeds in ownership of a like-kind property or several like-kind properties, thus, deferring the capital gains taxes. The 1031 is tax-deferred, meaning postponed, not tax-free. Consult with your CPA for specifics on 1031 exchanges and if they are the right choice for you.

Business Owner Tip: Make sure you declare your intentions for a 1031 to your title company prior to closing, otherwise you will lose the opportunity. There is NO option to retroactively engage a 1031 exchange after your property has closed.

The Next Chapter

While one dream has ended, another adventure awaits. If it is not another commercial building, enjoy the fruits of your labor and buy a custom RV and tour the country. Maybe sip Manhattans by the poolside while you remotely deposit that big fat check from your tenant. Perhaps 1031 exchange into an Airbnb property that you visit a few times a year while managing another revenue stream.

Me? When I sell my place, I'm going to build an art studio and design large mixed-medium sculptures—whatever inspires me in the moment. Now we're living!

APPENDIX 1

Terms and Definitions for Commercial Real Estate[1]

Construction Terminology: Build it, and They Will Come

Build-to-Suit: A building is designed and tailored for a specific tenant, often because the tenant is unable to find suitable space in the speculative market. Sometimes (but not always), a build-to-suit project includes specific design features not commonly found in the speculative market, thus, compelling the tenant to have a special facility built. The build-to-suit project is usually contracted with a developer who owns and operates the completed facility occupied by the tenant.

1 Maria Sicola, *Commercial Real Estate Terms and Definitions,* NAIOP Research Foundation, March 19www.naiop.org/globalassets/research-and-publications/report/terms-and-definitions-/researchreportcre-terms-and-definitions-2017.pdf.

Generally, a build-to-suit project becomes a single-tenant building upon completion.

Retrofit Modernization: For building systems such as heating, ventilation, and air conditioning (HVAC); security; fire alarms; and energy management. The tenant remains in the building, and the building use and square footage do not change. Retrofit is often done together with a renovation.

Under Renovation: A building is typically under renovation when construction permits have been obtained and demolition has begun. A building is under renovation if it remains inhabitable by tenants during the construction. If an existing building is gutted extensively (i.e., elevators and bathrooms do not function and it can, therefore, not be occupied by a tenant), then the building should be removed from inventory and redelivered when the occupancy permit is issued.

Building Terms and Definitions

Common Area: The building-wide accessible areas found on each floor of an office building such as washrooms, janitorial closets, electrical rooms, telephone rooms, mechanical rooms, elevator lobbies, and public corridors that are available for use by all tenants on that floor. It does not include major vertical penetrations such as elevator shafts, stairways, equipment runs, etc., (identified as a percentage of rentable area).

Core Area: The common area plus vertical penetrations in an office building measured in square feet. Core area is typically expressed as a percentage of net rentable area. This factor, which ranges from 5 to 20 percent for typical office buildings, can be computed for an entire building or a single floor of a building.

Floor Plate: The gross square footage of each floor in a multistory building. Individual floor plate sizes may vary according to the design of a building.

Functional Obsolescence: A descriptive term used to characterize a building that cannot be improved to meet current market standards or tastes without a complete replacement of buildings systems and finishes.

Load Factor or Core Factor: The load factor is calculated by dividing the rentable building area (RBA) by the usable area. This factor can then be applied to the usable area to convert it to RBA for comparison. In markets where space is leased on the basis of the usable area, if the load factor is 15 percent, then the usable area can be multiplied by 1.15, resulting in the RBA.

Loan to Value Ratio (LTV): The ratio between a mortgage loan and the value of the property pledged as security, usually expressed as a percentage.

Sale / Leaseback: An owner-occupied property that is sold to a third-party investor. The previous owner becomes the tenant that pays rent to the new owner. This tactic allows property owners to convert their ownership (equity) into cash while still occupying the property. The seller's (now the tenant's) lease term must be for two or more years.

Shell Space: Space within a property that is currently not built out.

Short Sale: When the sale price of an asset is less than the amount owed to the lender, and when the lender accepts this amount as full payment for the loan. Those funds not repaid to the lender will be written off.

Sublet Space: Space offered for lease indirectly by a tenant rather than directly by a landlord.

Year Built: The year the building was delivered to the market as a result of completed construction.

Year Renovated: The year the building last received a Certificate of Occupancy (C of O) for a major renovation.

1031 Exchange or Like-kind Exchange: U.S. Internal Revenue Code Section 1031 permits the deferral of capital gains taxes on the sale of property held for investment or productive use in a trade or a business. With a 1031 exchange, property owners can sell their real estate, and then reinvest the proceeds in ownership of a like-kind property or several like-kind properties, thus, deferring the capital gains taxes. The like-kind exchange under Section 1031 is tax-deferred, not tax-free. When the replacement property is ultimately sold (not as part of another exchange), the original deferred gain, plus any additional gain realized since the purchase of the replacement property, is subject to tax.

Office Building-related Definitions

When purchasing office space, you may encounter the terms below. The office terminology section is a collection of essential and commonly used terms describing various types of office space—often identified by the type(s) of tenants occupying the space. This section captures definitions around the current trends impacting the sector, such as shared office space and more traditional terms like "space classification."

Creative Office Space: Previously industrial space with high ceilings and exposed air ducts. The space is often made of brick and timber and has been converted to office or studio space that often caters to technology, advertising, media, and entertainment tenants (TAME).

Medical Office Building: (MOB) A structure with at least 75 percent of its interior built out to accommodate healthcare providers, such as doctors and dentists or healthcare technicians who perform exams with specialized equipment. Typically, the buildings have more robust mechanical, electrical, and plumbing systems as well as reinforced floors to accommodate numerous exam rooms and heavy medical equipment.

Multitenant Office Building: A building that is not owner occupied and space that is leased to two or more tenants. As an owner/user you may want a property with additional income, such as a multitenant office building.

Office Building: A structure providing environments that are conducive to the performance of management and administrative activities, accounting, marketing, information processing, consulting, human resources management, financial and insurance services, educational and medical services, and other professional services.

Office Condo: Short for "office condominium," this term refers to the ownership structure of an office property in which individual units housed in one structure are sold to independent owners. Typically, there are covenants that govern the activities that can be carried out and improvements that can be made to each unit. These covenants also stipulate the distribution of costs related to the maintenance and operations of common elements in the building, such as the roof and the elevators.

Office Park or Office Campus: Contiguous acres of land, master-planned with roads, sidewalks, trails, and extensive landscaping that accommodate stand-alone office buildings with adjacent surface parking lots or parking structures.

Owner-occupied Office Building: Buildings that are occupied by the owner and that generally are not included in the competitive inventory.

Single-tenant Office Building: A building for which there is a single lease obligation.

Stacking Plan: A floor-by-floor and suite-by-suite graphical representation of each floor and suite within a building. The plan shows the suite number, the square footage of each suite, and the tenant occupying each. On many stacking plans, lease expiration dates are also provided to give a quick view of the occupancy exposure within a building.

Industrial Building-related Definitions

When buying warehouse space, you may encounter these terms outlined below. The industrial real estate vocabulary section includes definitions, characteristics, and features of the major industrial product types.

Apron: The area, within the truck court, where trucks are parked for loading and unloading. This area will be paved with more durable material than will the rest of the truck court (e.g., concrete or other structural reinforcement versus asphalt) to withstand the heavy loads being parked there.

Automobile Parking Ratio: A ratio calculated by comparing the number of automobile parking spaces at a project to the gross leasable area (GLA) of a building. This ratio is usually expressed in number of spaces per 1,000 square feet of gross leasable space. It varies by property use, with labor-intensive operations needing higher parking ratios. For example, a building with a GLA of 800,000 SF would have 800 spaces expressed as eight spaces/1,000 SF.

Bay Depth: The distance between columns. (Synonyms: clear span, column spacing.)

Bay Width: The distance from one side of the bay to the other.

Biotech Space Highly: Specialized laboratory or research and development space. The space is uniquely configured and is typically developed to the needs of the biotech tenant. It may require significant retrofit should the tenant vacate the space. The space is often characterized by robust mechanical, electrical, and plumbing systems, as well as by sophisticated ventilation systems to accommodate the highly specialized and complex activities that occur inside and that involve the handling of chemicals, drugs, and biological matter.

Cantilever Rack: Racking system containing shelving supports that are connected to vertical supports at the rear of the rack. This type of rack is used for storing long material, such as lumber and piping.

Ceiling Height: Distance from the floor to the inside overhead upper surface of the room. This measure will be higher than any hanging objects, beams, joists, or trusses, unless there is a suspended ceiling. This differs from clear height.

Clear Height: Distance from the floor to the lowest hanging ceiling member or hanging objects, beams, joists, or truss work descending down into a substantial portion of the industrial work area. This is the most important measure of the interior height of an industrial building because it defines the minimum height of usable space within the structure. (Synonyms: clear headway, clearance.)

Clear Span: An open area with no obstructions.

Column Spacing: The distance between posts or vertical supporting beams in a building.

Cross Dock Loading: Docks on opposite sides of a relatively shallow distribution facility that allow for quick loading, sorting, or unloading from one vehicle to another (i.e., materials from one truck at a loading dock are unloaded, sorted, and reloaded onto one or more trucks).

Distribution Building: A type of warehouse facility designed to accommodate efficient movement of goods.

Dock-high Door: A loading dock door that is not at ground level, but rather, is elevated to four feet to be even with the standard tractor-trailer height for loading or unloading goods without a change in elevation. Some doors, called "semi dock" or "half dock," are constructed at a two-foot height to accommodate smaller or lower delivery trucks.

Door-to-square-foot Ratio: The ratio of the total number of loading docks and drive-in doors to the building's total square feet.

Drive-in Door: A door through which trucks, forklifts, and other machinery or vehicles can enter and exit without a change in elevation.

Flex Facility: As its name suggests, an industrial building designed to be used in a variety of ways. It is usually located in an industrial park setting. Specialized flex buildings can include service centers, showrooms, offices, warehouses, and more.

High Cube: A relative term that refers to industrial buildings with an abundance of clear height or vertical cubic space. (Synonym: high bay.)

Industrial Building: A structure used primarily for manufacturing, research and development, production, maintenance, and storage or distribution of goods, or both. It can include some office space. Industrial buildings are divided into three primary classifications: manufacturing, warehouse or distribution, and flex.

Leveler: Steel plates that are moved by auto-hydraulic lifts to make a loading dock level with a truck bed. A fully loaded truck may sit four to six inches lower than a standard forty-eight-inch-high dock. The device is used to account for the difference so a forklift can be driven in and out of a truck. A building equipped with multiple loading docks may not have a leveler for each dock.

Loading Dock: An elevated platform at the shipping or delivery door of a building, usually situated at the same height as the floor of a shipping container on a truck or railroad car to facilitate loading and unloading. Loading docks can also be exterior ramps covered with a canopy or some element that protects the loading area from the elements. Otherwise, they can be flush with the exterior of the building and accessed through a sliding door adjacent to the interior of the building.

Mezzanine Office: Office space that is built in an industrial facility. It is usually along the perimeter of a facility and creates an intermediate floor.

Office Percentage: The percentage of total square feet in an industrial building that is built for use as office space. When the mezzanine office is built above a space that would otherwise be an industrial work area, this additional square footage is not counted in the total square footage of the building.

Push-back Rack Racking: A system with a sliding device that pushes back pallets, thereby allowing multiple pallets to be placed in the same location.

Radio Frequency Identification: (RFID) Inventory-tracking technology embedded in devices that are attached to package labels so an item's location can be tracked.

Rail Door: A door that is generally side loading, that has access to railroad tracks, to facilitate the loading or unloading of goods from a railroad car to an industrial building.

Rail Service: A railroad spur adjacent to a building structure that allows the building to be served by rail operations.

Ramp Door: A dock-high door that has been converted to a drive-in door by creating a ramp from ground level to dock level.

Side-loading Dock: A loading dock configuration designed to facilitate the loading and unloading of a vehicle through its side.

Super Flat Floors: Concrete floors with minimal variations in elevation from point to point. The floors are found primarily in warehouses with automated systems. Precisely calibrated and leveled picking machinery and racks require level flooring to ensure proper operation.

Truck Court: Exterior area adjacent to an industrial building's loading docks where trucks maneuver. The most important measure of the truck court is the depth from the building to the end of the truck court. Greater depth allows for greater maneuverability and better accommodates multiple trucks.

Truck Terminal: This specialized distribution building for redistributing goods from one truck to another, serves as an intermediate transfer point. The facilities are primarily used for staging loads (rather than long-term storage) and possess very little, if any, storage area.

Truck-turning Radius: The tightest turn a truck can make, depending on several variables such as truck configuration, trailer size, and location of adjacent objects, that obstructs the inner turning radius. Truss A framework of beams forming a rigid structure (as in a roof truss).

Truss Height: Distance from the floor to the bottom edge of a truss used to support the ceiling or roof of a building. If there are hanging objects, beams, or joists below the truss, the clear height will be lower than the truss height.

APPENDIX 2

Nine-Step Guideline and Timeline for Purchasing a Commercial Building

☐ **Step One:** Strategic plan, the power of preparation (one to two hours). Meet the buyer rep to discuss your buying parameters, lease versus purchase, and define a plan of action.

☐ **Step Two:** Identify potential properties (one to three days). Review property options that match your building parameters, select properties to tour, and set the tour date.

☐ **Step Three:** Property tour, seeing is believing. (Estimate thirty minutes per property.) Tour properties and take notes for discussion.

☐ **Step Four:** Patience, the letter of intent (up to two weeks). Strategize and understand the letter of intent terms before presenting to the seller.

- [ ] **Step Five:** The lender and due diligence. (Start the lending process any time during the transaction, yet earlier is prudent.) What lenders require, and why.
- [ ] **Step Six:** The title company. Purchase contract negotiations and open escrow (from signing the PSA through the closing of the property). Once the purchase contract is negotiated and executed by both parties, escrow is opened, and the purchase timeline starts ticking.
- [ ] **Step Seven:** Redesign and construction bids (two to four weeks). This process usually commences once escrow has opened and continues during the due diligence period. It often overlaps with the closing period as well.
- [ ] **Step Eight:** The home stretch, the close (fifteen to forty-five days after the expiration of due diligence). Title and lender prepare closing documents for review by seller and buyer.
- [ ] **Step Nine:** Ownership, one task at a time. It is time to commence construction or move into your new property. Congratulations!

APPENDIX 3

Buyer Purchase Matrix
(A downloadable version is at www.davisCREAZ.com)

BUYER BROKER REPRESENTATION
1. Research and analyses property(s) and sets tour.
2. Writes initial offer (LOI-letter of intent.)
3. Negotiates LOI with buyer for Purchase Contract (PSA.)
4. Reviews PSA against LOI terms and sends to attorney to comment.
5. Facilitates information flow between all parties.
6. Coordinates inspections and is ideally present for them.
7. Gathers due diligence materials and reviews with client.
8. May create check list and 'to do' list for client.
9. Provides reliable referrals such as attorney, architect, contractor, etc.
10. Assures everyone plays nice in the sandbox through closing.

TITLE RESPONSIBILITIES
1. Opens escrow and holds earnest monies.
2. Issues title commitment and Schedule B.
3. May prepare a critical dates reference sheet.
4. Handles any title buyer/seller objections.
5. Issues settlement statement prior to closing.
6. Coordinates 1031 exchange documents with qualified intermediary.
7. Prepares and distributes closing documents to all parties.
8. Makes sure documents related to the transaction are signed.
   Example: estoppel. SNDA (Subordination and Non-Disturbance Agreement)
   and Assignment of Leases – for investment only.
9. Note: an ALTA survey is required for an extended title warranty.

CPA/FINANCIAL PLANNER QUESTIONS
1. Is this a 1031 tax deferred exchange property?
2. Should you do cost segregation for tenant improvements?
3. What is the best way to take title? LLC, Family Trust...
4. What is your exit strategy?

PROPERTY INSPECTIONS
1. Building Inspection
2. Appraisal
3. ALTA Survey
4. Environmental Report or Phase I
} Lender may require

CONTRACTOR (TI's)
1. Tours building with buyer.
2. Offers cost saving suggestions.
3. Provides remodel estimate.

PROPERTY

LENDER REQUIREMENTS
1. Interview multiple lenders.
2. Buyer financials.
3. Property information.
4. Signed PSA and title contact.
5. Property requirements:
   a. Appraisal
   b. Phase I or environmental report
   c. ALTA survey of the property boundaries

ATTORNEY ASSISTANCE
1. Drafts/reviews PSA and finalizes negotiations.
2. Helps review title info and Schedule B.
3. Writes title objections.
4. Answers legal questions related to due diligence documents.
5. If necessary, drafts any PSA amendments.
6. For investment properties with tenants in place
   see Investment Property section.

INVESTMENT PROPERTY
1. Assess tenant financials.
2. Review lease(s) – you're buying the tenants' financial strength.
3. Review service contracts on property.
4. Ask for proof of rent payment, actual invoices.
5. Keep earnest monies refundable until estoppel certificates are reviewed.
6. Signed estoppels required and tenant SNDA.

NEGOTIATION OPPORTUNITIES
1. Initial offer – LOI basic deal terms.
2. PSA review – legal language.
3. Post building inspections.
4. Post appraisal.
5. After any unusual findings during due diligence.

Subjective buyer's purchase matrix compiled from years of transactions. There are always more than one way to close a CRE deal. Remember to consult your real estate professional, attorney, CPA, financial planner, etc. when purchasing commercial real estate. Enjoy the process.

APPENDIX 4
Checklist for Hiring a Buyer Rep

☐ Talk about the broker's current market knowledge from peers and recent transactions.

☐ Ask what analytics the buyer rep has access to.

☐ Ask to see a lease versus purchase analysis for discussion purposes.

☐ Request examples of how the broker negotiates the deal.

☐ Decipher if the broker can close the deal.

☐ Ascertain if the broker has significant knowledge in your type of building purchase.

☐ Discover how many commercial real estate sales the broker has closed over their career.

☐ Ask for credentials, and Google them to find out about their reputation.

☐ Avoid brokers who only show properties listed by their firm. Be wary if the only properties shown advertise incentives.

☐ Resist hiring a residential real estate agent when buying commercial properties.

APPENDIX 5
Checklist for Hiring a Real-Estate Attorney

☐ Verify the attorney specializes in commercial real estate in your state.

☐ Google the attorney's level of experience, and personally ask them about their knowledge.

☐ Ask for references.

☐ Request their hourly rate.

☐ Ask for an estimated time requirement to review the PSA, the title commitment report (Schedule B, in particular), and some due diligence items.

☐ Question when they can start working for you.

APPENDIX 6
Top Buyer Mistakes When Purchasing a Building

☐ Underestimating the value of a commercial real
estate broker.

☐ Hiring a residential broker versus a commercial broker.

☐ Low balling the initial offer to see how the seller responds.
This puts the seller on the defensive, and negotiations only
go downhill from there.

☐ Not hiring an attorney for legal advice throughout the
process because you assume the fee is too expensive.

☐ Insisting on closing early when due diligence
isn't complete.

☐ Rushing the process.

www.ingramcontent.com/pod-product-compliance
Lightning Source LLC
Chambersburg PA
CBHW020907180526
45163CB00007B/2649